Everything ~~y~~
always wanted to know about

WOODY ALLEN

FRANK WEIMANN

SHAPOLSKY PUBLISHERS, INC.
New York

A Shapolsky Book
Copyright © 1991 by Frank Weimann

All rights reserved under International and Pan American Copyright Conventions. Published in the U.S.A. by Shapolsky Publishers, Inc. No parts of this book may be used or reproduced in any manner whatsoever without written permission of Shapolsky Publishers, Inc., except in the case of brief quotations embodied in critical articles or reviews.

For any additional information, contact:
Shapolsky Publishers, Inc.
136 West 22nd Street, New York, NY 10011
(212) 633-2022

1 2 3 4 5 6 7 8 9 10

Library of Congress Cataloging-in-Publication Data

Cover photograph and all internal photographs courtesy of Brian Hamill

ISBN 1-56171-017-2

Printed and bound by Graficromo s.a., Cordoba, Spain

For my father
who never had the opportunity
to see a Woody Allen film
and for my daughter, Victoria
who will

I would like to thank my mother, Natalie Weimann and my sisters Lee, Linda and Marlene for all their emotional support and Art (for his financial support) while I agonized over this project. Brian (a stranger here in town) Rago and the gorgeous Natalie Rago. George Spohn, thanks for bailing me out so often over the years and for your friendship, which I value very much. Lisa Aloisi for helping me get this book off the notepad and onto the computer. Special thanks to the Taylor's, who allowed me to "hang around their house" when I started this book. To fellow Woody Allen fanatic, Harlan "Al Singer" Coben, Eric (d.c.) Todd and the guys from Danger Danger.

Contents

The Books
Questions

1. In which book was "The UFO Menace"
    published?

    a) *Getting Even*
    b) *Side Effects*
    c) *Without Feathers*
    d) *The Sky's the Limit*

2. Match the short story with the magazine in
    which it first appeared:

    "A Twenties Memory"
    "Death Knocks"
    "The Irish Genius"
    "The Discovery of the Fake Ink Blot"
    "Yes, But Can Steam Engines Do This"

a) *New Republic*
b) *New Yorker*
c) *Playboy*
d) *Reader's Digest*
e) *Saturday Evening Post*

3. When "F" broke his diet his father:

a) Approved of his homosexual marriage
b) Condemned him to death
c) Kissed him on the lips
d) Threw him out of the house

4. According to "Getting Even," what are you no longer permitted to do once you're accepted into the mob?

a) Eat fig newtons
b) Imitate a hen
c) Kill anyone name Carlo
d) All of the above

5. Certain comic bits in "Retribution" and "The Lunatic's Tale" are seen in which of the following movies?

a) *Bananas*
b) *Purple Rose of Cairo*
c) *Sleeper*
d) *Stardust Memories*

6. The Whore of Mensa got busted for:

a) Attending graduate school at NYU
b) Discussing "The Cat in the Hat Comes Back" with a total stranger
c) Reading *Commentary* in a parked car
d) Writing a novelization of *All the President's Men*

7.   In "The Spring Bulletin's Introduction to Social Work," topics include:

   a) How to organize gangs into basketball teams and vice versa
   b) How to sing do wop music as a means of escape
   c) What octave to hit when smacked in the head with a bicycle chain
   d) The playground guide to tooth extraction

8.   "Death Knocks" is a takeoff on:

   a) Bergman's *The Seventh Seal*
   b) Chaplin's *City Lights*
   c) Fellini's *Amarcord*
   d) Guccione's *September Issue*

9.   In "The UFO Menace," Gus was injected with a fluid that caused him to do what?

   a) Hop around on one foot and yell "toodles!"
   b) Smile and act like Bopeep
   c) Sing "The Battle Hymn of the Republic"
   d) Suffer a nervous breakdown that made him incapable of conversing unless using a hand puppet

10.   "A Guide to Some of the Lesser Ballets" includes:

   a) Dmitri, The Sacrifice and The Hairball
   b) Gomer, Mother Knows Best and The Degenerate
   c) The Spell, The Predators and A Day in the Life of a Doe
   d) Otherness, Social Deviate and For Crying Out Loud

11. True or False:

    a) *Without Feathers* was published in 1976.

    b) "Count Dracula" won the O. Henry award for best short story in 1977.

    c) In "A Look at Organized Crime," Little Tony was also known as Rabbi Henry Sharpstein.

12. In what book did each of the following short stories appear:

"Hassidic Tales"	a) *Getting Even*
"No Kaddish for Weinstein"	b) *Side Effects*
"Remembering Needleman"	c) *Without Feathers*

13. The title *Without Feathers* is derived from a poem from what great poet?

    a) E.E. Cummings

    b) Emily Dickinson

    c) Henry Wadsworth Longfellow

    d) Walt Whitman

14. How did Inspector Ford solve "The Macabre Accident"?

    a) He knew that an experienced hunter would not stalk game in his underwear.

    b) There was a copy of *Field and Stream* nearby.

    c) He had been playing the spoons.

    d) All of the above.

15. Miscellaneous methods of "Civil Disobedience" include:

   a) Pretending to be a sea mollusk
   b) Not brushing your teeth for 6 months
   c) Dressing up as a policeman and then skipping
   d) Taking a mortgage out on a pretzel

16. "Fabrizio's: Criticism and Response" is a rebuttal to the critics of which film?

   a) *Interiors*
   b) *Love and Death*
   c) *Midsummer's Night Sex Comedy*
   d) *Stardust Memories*

17. In "Fine Times: An Oral Memoir," Ned Small was machine-gunned to death for what reason?

   a) Saying the word "Kleenex" repeatedly
   b) Spilling raisins on Al Capone's hat
   c) Transporting white socks over state lines for immoral purposes
   d) Committing an adulterous act with a penguin

18. Topics in "Economic Theory" include:

   a) Interest, loans and welching
   b) How to construct a skyscraper on the bridge of someone's nose
   c) Obstacles to overcome when financing a sandwich
   d) Purchasing a wildebeest at wholesale prices

19. Sandor Needleman eloquently argued that true evil could only be perpetrated by:

a) Nazis
b) His landlord
c) Someone named Blackie or Pete
d) His ex-wife

20. Weinstein was positive that collectivization would work if everyone:

a) Believed in communism
b) Learned the lyrics to "I Enjoy Being a Girl"
c) Sharpened their noses with pumice
d) Smeared their bodies with chives

The Books
Answers

1. b) *Side Effects*

2. "A Twenties Memory"   e)
    "Death Knocks   b)
    "The Irish Genius"   a)
    "The Discovery of the Fake
        Ink Blot"   c)
    "Yes, But Can Steam Engines
        Do This"   d)

3. b) Condemned him to death

4. b) Imitate a hen

5. d) *Stardust Memories*

6. c) Reading *Commentary* in a parked car

7. a) How to organize gangs into basketball teams and vice versa

8. a) Bergman's *The Seventh Seal*

9. b) Smile and act like Bopeep

10. c) The Spell, The Predators, and A Day in the Life of a Doe

11. a) False
    b) False
    c) True

12. a) *Getting Even*
    b) *Without Feathers*
    c) *Side Effects*

13. b) Emily Dickinson

14. d) All of the above

15. c) Dressing up as a policeman and then skipping

16. a) *Interiors*

17. b) Spilling raisins on Al Capone's hat

18. a) Interest, loans and welching

19. c) Someone named Blackie or Pete

20. b) Learned the lyrics to "I Enjoy Being a Girl"

The Plays
Questions

1. Who played Enid Pollack?

    a) Bea Arthur
    b) Colleen Dewhurst
    c) George Maharis
    d) Maureen Stapleton

2. Who played Nancy in the stage version of *Play It Again, Sam*?

    a) Susan Anspach
    b) Rock Hudson
    c) Diane Keaton
    d) Shelia Sullivan

3.   At which theatre did each of the plays open?

Don't Drink the Water   a)   Broadhurst
Play It Again, Sam   b)   Morosco
The Floating Lightbulb   c)   Vivian Beaumont

4   Who does not appear in *"The Floating
      Lightbulb"*?

      a)   Danny Aiello
      b)   Beatrice Arthur
      c)   Thomas Edison
      d)   Jack Weston

5.   Who did not appear in *"Don't Drink
      the Water"*?

      a)   Lou Jacobi
      b)   Ralph Kramden
      c)   Donna Mills
      d)   Tony Roberts

6.   Who did not appear in *"Play It Again, Sam"*

      a)   Diane Keaton
      b)   Jerry Lacy
      c)   Michael Murphy
      d)   Tony Roberts

7.   _____was the setting for
      "The Floating Lightbulb".

      a)   Canarsie, Brooklyn
      b)   Forest Hills, Queens
      c)   San Francisco, CA
      d)   Sheepshead Bay, Brooklyn

8.   *Don't Drink the Water* ran for how
        many performances?

        a) 345
        b) 435
        c) 598
        d) 895

9.   What makes October, 1969 significant?

        a) It's the day Woody's mother had her
            hysterectomy.
        b) New Kids On The Block wouldn't sing
            for another 20 years.
        c) *Play It Again, Sam* opened.
        d) Pope's wife gave birth to triplets.

10.   Who directed *Don't Drink the Water?*

        a) Woody Allen
        b) David Merrick
        c) Stanley Prager
        d) Jack Rollins

The Plays
Answers

1. a) Bea Arthur

2. d) Shelia

3. b) *Don't Drink the Water*
    a) *Play It Again, Sam*
    c) *The Floating Lightbulb*

4. c) Thomas Edison

5. b) Ralph Kramden

6. c) Michael Murphy

7. a) Carnarsie

8. c) 598

9. c) *Play It Again, Sam* opened

10. c) Stanley Prager

General Movie Information Questions

1. Gershwin music is to *Manhattan* as Mendelssohn music is to:

    a) *A Midsummer's Night Sex Comedy*
    b) *Love and Death*
    c) *Purple Rose of Cairo*
    d) *September*

2. What film parallels Bergman's *Seventh Seal*?

    a) *A Midsummer's Night Sex Comedy*
    b) *Interiors*
    c) *Love and Death*
    d) *Stardust Memories*

3.   In what film did Karen Ludwig have an important role?

    a) *A Midsummer's Night Sex Comedy*
    b) *Manhattan*
    c) *Purple Rose of Cairo*
    d) *The Front*

4.   Match the character with their dialogue:

    a) "I can't suck anybody's leg that I'm not engaged to."
    b) "I need a valium the size of a hockey puck."
    c) "I never want rabbit—I don't eat rodent."
    d) "Tonight, I think I'll brush all of my teeth."

Sandy Bates   Fielding Mellish
Alan Felix   Danny Rose

5.   In what two films does Woody Allen portray Victor Shakapopolis?

    a) *Casino Royale* and *Everything You Always Wanted to Know about Sex*
    b) *What's Up Tiger Lily?* and *What's New Pussycat?*
    c) *Everything You Always Wanted to Know about Sex* and *What's New Pussycat?*
    d) *The Front* and *What's New Pussycat?*

6. The National Catholic Office for Motion Pictures gave which film a condemned rating?

    a) *Bananas*
    b) *Everything You Always Wanted to Know about Sex*
    c) *Interiors*
    d) *Take the Money and Run*

7. What movie did Vincent Canby of the New York *Times* describe as "marvelous and sometimes breathtaking in its effects"?

    a) *Annie Hall*
    b) *Hannah and Her Sisters*
    c) *Love and Death*
    d) *Stardust Memories*

8. Match the character with his profession:

    a) Alan   Clerk
    b) Andrew   Film critic
    c) Howard   Restaurant cashier
    d) Isaac   Stockbroker
    e) Leonard   TV producer
    f) Mickey   TV writer

9. There is an obvious parody of Eisenstein's *Potemkin* in which film?

    a) *Bananas*
    b) *Love and Death*
    c) *Take the Money and Run*
    d) a and b
    e) b and c

10. "Let's Misbehave" was featured in what soundtrack?

    a) *Everything You Always Wanted to Know about Sex*
    b) *Radio Days*
    c) *Take the Mondy and Run*
    d) *Zelig*

11. Match the director with his film:

    a) Woody Allen   *Bananas*
    b) Clive Donner   *Casino Royale*
    c) John Huston   *Play It Again, Sam*
    d) Martin Ritt   *The Front*
    e) Herbert Ross   *What's New Pussycat?*

12. The "shaving-cream man from outerspace" is in what film?

    a) *Broadway Danny Rose*
    b) *Sleeper*
    c) *Stardust Memories*
    d) *What's Up Tiger Lily?*

13. In which of the following films did Diane Wiest appear?

    a) *Interiors*
    b) *The Purple Rose of Cairo*
    c) *Stardust Memories*
    d) *The Front*

14 "Marriage is the death of hope" was spoken in:

    a) *A Midsummer's Night Sex Comedy*
    b) *Broadway Danny Rose*
    c) *Interiors*
    d) *Stardust Memories*

18

15. The actor who portrayed Sandy Bates's brother-in-law Sam appeared in what other Film?

    a) *Hannah and Her Sisters*
    b) *Interiors*
    c) *Manhattan*
    d) *Radio Days*

16. What's the actor's name?

    a) John Doumanian
    b) Richard Jordan
    c) Jacqui Safra
    d) Daniel Stern

17. What film had the working title *Anhedonia*?

    a) *Annie Hall*
    b) *Hannah and Her Sisters*
    c) *Manhattan*
    d) *The Purple Rose of Cairo*

18. What is "Anhedonia"?

    a) An advanced masturbation technique
    b) The inability to experience pleasure
    c) Diane Keaton's middle name
    d) None of the above

19. Match the character with her movie:

Ariel	Helen	Pam
Ceil	Lee	Renata
Dorrie	Linda	Rita
Emma	Louise	Sonia
Eudora	Luna	Tina
Florence	Nancy	Tracy

19

a) *A Midsummer's Night Sex Comedy*
b) *Annie Hall*
c) *Bananas*
d) *Broadway Danny Rose*
e) *Everything You Always Wanted to Know...*
f) *Hannah and Her Sisters*
g) *Interiors*
h) *Love and Death*
i) *Manhattan*
j) *Play It Again, Sam*
k) *Radio Days*
l) *Sleeper*
m) *Stardust Memories*
n) *Take the Money and Run*
o) *The Front*
p) *Purple Rose of Cairo*
q) *What's New Pussycat?*
r) *Zelig*

20. Match the song with the movie soundtrack:

"A Hard Way to Go"
"Embraceable You"
"I Remember You"
"One O'clock Jump"
"Wolverine Blues"
"Young at Heart"

a) *Annie Hall*
b) *Hannah and Her Sisters*
c) *Interiors*
d) *Manhattan*
e) *Stardust Memories*
f) *The Front*

21.   Who said, "Our society places a great value
       on jokes"?

       a)   Sandy Bates
       b)   Isaac Davis
       c)   Howard Prince
       d)   Alvy Singer

22.   In what film(s) does Woody portray a character
       named Felix?

       a)   *Casino Royale*
       b)   *Everything You Always Wanted to Know
            about Sex*
       c)   *Play It Again, Sam*
       d)   *What's New Pussycat?*

23.   In what movie do you hear, "You look in the
       mirror and see that there's something miss-
       ing...then you realize it's your future"?

       a)   *A Midsummer's Night Sex Comedy*
       b)   *Hannah and Her Sisters*
       c)   *Interiors*
       d)   *September*

24.   Match the composer and the film:

       Burt Bacharach   Marvin Hamlisch
       Billy Goldenberg   Mundell Lowe
       Dave Grusin

       a)   *Bananas*
       b)   *Everything You Always Wanted to Know...*
       c)   *Play It Again, Sam*
       d)   *The Front*
       e)   *What's New Pussycat?*

25   Match the film with the director of photography:

Bananas
Everything You Always Wanted to Know...
Interiors
Love and Death
Play It Again, Sam
Take the Money and Run
The Front

a) Michael Chapman
b) Ghislain Cloquet
c) Andrew Costikyan
d) Owen Roizman
e) Lester Shorr
f) David Walsh
g) Gordon Willis

26.   Match the movie with the year released

a) *A Midsummer's Night Sex Comedy* 1965
b) *Annie Hall* 1966
b) *Another Woman* 1967
d) *Bananas* 1969
e) *Broadway Danny Rose* 1971
f) *Casino Royale* 1972
g) *Crimes and Misdemeanors* 1973
h) *Everything You Always* 1973
i) *Hannah and Her Sisters* 1975
j) *Interiors* 1976
k) *Love & Death* 1977
l) *Manhattan* 1978
m) *New York Stories* 1979

n) *Play It Again, Sam*   1980
o) *Radio Days*   1982
p) *Sleeper*   1983
q) *Stardust Memories*   1984
r) *Take the Money and Run*   1985
s) *The Front*   1986
t) *The Purple Rose of Cairo*   1987
u) *What's New Pussycat?*   1988
v) *What's Up Tiger Lilly?*   1989
w) *Zelig*   1989

27.   Match the character with his movie:

Sandy Bates   Fielding Mellish
Jimmy Bonds   Miles Monroe
Isaac Davis   Howard Prince
Alan Felix   Victor Shakapopolis
Boris Grushenko   Virgil Starkwell

a) *Bananas*
b) *Casino Royale*
c) *Love & Death*
d) *Manhattan*
e) *Play It Again, Sam*
f) *Sleeper*
g) *Stardust Memories*
h) *Take the Money and Run*
i) *The Front*
j) *What's New Pussycat?*

28.   Julie Kavners first appearance in
       a Woody Allen film was:

a) *Interiors*
b) *Hannah & Her Sisters*
c) *Radio Days*
d) *Zelig*

29. Danny Aiello appears in *Radio Days* and what other Allen film?

  a) *A Midsummer's Night Sex Comedy*
  b) *Hannah and Her Sisters*
  c) *September*
  d) *The Purple Rose of Cairo*

30. A character named Nat Bernstein is seen or spoken about in what film(s)?

  a) *Interiors*
  b) *Radio Days*
  c) *Stardust Memories*
  d) b and c

31. A request for a sock with horse manure is made in:

  a) *Bananas/Annie Hall*
  b) *Manhattan/Sleeper*
  c) *Radio Days/Annie Hall*
  d) *Take the Money and Run/Annie Hall*

32. The original ending of which film was extremely violent?

  a) *Bananas*
  b) *Love and Death*
  c) *Stardust Memories*
  d) *Take the Money and Run*

33. Match the phrases with the film:

  a) "Arlene thinks I'm a pervert because I drank our waterbed."

b) "We all want what we can't have in life, it's an actual thing."

c) "Put down that gun; she's over eighteen."

d) "I don't know if you remember me but we had the worst day of my life together."

Broadway Danny Rose   Love and Death
Hannah and Her Sisters   Sleeper

34. "I'm like a cat, I'll always wind up on my feet" is said in how many films?

a) None
b) One
c) Two
d) Three

35. Name them.

36. Louise Lasser appears in or is some way involved in how many Woody Allen films?

37. Name them.

38. Although eventually edited out, Woody's father was originally a taxi driver in which of the following movies?

a) *Annie Hall*
b) *Bananas*
c) *Hannah and Her Sisters*
d) *The Front*

39.　Gordon Willis was the director of photography for which of the following?

　　a)　*Hannah and Her Sisters*
　　b)　*Radio Days*
　　c)　*September*
　　d)　None of the above
　　e)　All of the above

40.　Long considered the finest still photographer in the industry, Brian Hamill has worked with Woody Allen since this film.

　　a)　*A Midsummer's Night Sex Comedy*
　　b)　*Annie Hall*
　　c)　*Bananas*
　　d)　*Crimes and Misdemeanors*

General Movie Information
Answers

1.   a) *A Midsummer's Night Sex Comedy*

2.   c) *Love and Death*

3.   b) *Manhattan*

4.   a) Fielding Mellish
        b) Danny Rose
        c) Sandy Bates
        d) Alan Felix

5.   c) *Everything You Always Wanted to Know about Sex* and *What's New Pussycat?*

6.   a) *Bananas*

7.   d) *Stardust Memories*

8.   a) Film Critic
     b) Stockbroker
     c) Restaurant cashier
     d) TV writer
     e) Clerk
     f) TV producer

9.   d) a and b

10. a) *Everything You Always Wanted to Know about Sex*

11. a) *Bananas*
     b) *What's new Pussycat?*
     c) *Casino Royale*
     d) *The Front*
     e) *Play It Again, Sam*

12. a) *Broadway Danny Rose*

13. b) *The Purple Rose of Cairo*

14. a) *A Midsummer's Night Sex Comedy*

15. d) *Radio Days*

16. c) Jacqui Safra

17. a) *Annie Hall*

18. b) The inability to experience pleasure

19. a) Ariel   g) Renata   m) Dorrie
    b) Pam   h) Sonia   n) Louise
    c) Nancy   i) Tracy   o) Florence
    d) Tina   j) Linda   p) Emma
    e) Helen   k) Ceil   q) Rita
    f) Lee   l) Luna   r) Eudora

20. a) "A Hard Way to Go"
    b) "I Remember You"
    c) "Wolverine Blues"
    d) "Embraceable You"
    e) "One O'clock Jump"
    f) "Young at Heart"

21. a) Sandy Bates

22. e) *What's New Pussycat?*

23. d) *September*

24. a) Marvin Hamlisch
    b) Mundell Lowe
    c) Billy Goldenberg
    d) Dave Grusin
    e) Burt Bacharach

25. a) *The Front*
    b) *Love and Death*
    c) *Bananas*
    d) *Play It Again, Sam*
    e) *Take the Money and Run*
    f) *Everything You Always...*
    g) *Interiors*

General Movie Information—Answers

26.   a) 1982   h) 1978   o) 1969
      b) 1977   i) 1975   p) 1976
      c) 1971   j) 1979   q) 1985
      d) 1984   k) 1972   r) 1965
      e) 1967   l) 1987   s) 1966
      f) 1972   m) 1973   t) 1983
      g) 1986   n) 1980

27.   a) Fielding Mellish
      b) Jimmy Bonds
      c) Boris Grushenko
      d) Isaac Davis
      e) Alan Felix
      f) Miles Monroe
      g) Sandy Bates
      h) Virgil Starkwell
      i) Howard Prince
      j) Victor Shakapopolis

28.   b) *Hannah and Her Sisters*

29.   d) *The Purple Rose of Cairo*

30.   d) b and c

31.   c) *Radio Days/Annie Hall*

32.   d) *Take the Money and Run*

33.   a) *Sleeper*
      b) *Broadway Danny Rose*
      c) *Love and Death*
      d) *Hannah and Her Sisters*

34.   c) Two

35.   *Bananas/Sleeper*

36.   Six

37.   *Stardust, Everything You Always, Bananas, Take the Money, What's Up Tiger?, What's New Pussycat?*

38.   a) *Annie Hall*

39.   d) All of the above

40.   b) Annie Hall

Apprenticeship–
The Early Movies
Questions

What's New Pussycat? **(1965),** *What's Up Tiger Lily?*
(1966), *Casino Royale* **(1967)**

1.   Who was the hero in *What's Up Tiger Lily?*

    a)   Phil Moscowitz
    b)   Howard Prince
    c)   Victor Shakapopolis
    d)   Shemp Howard

2.   Who did not appear in *What's New Pussycat?*

    a)   Ursula Andress
    b)   Britt Ekland
    c)   Peter Sellers
    d)   Peter O'Toole

3. Woody avoided any and all participation in the film:

    a) *Casino Royale*
    b) *Don't Drink the Water*
    c) *What's New Pussycat?*
    d) *What's Up Tiger Lily*

4. True or false:

    a) It is written that he who has the best recipe for egg salad shall rule the world.
    b) Fritz Fassbinder was a psychiatrist.
    c) Hollander told Axel that years of insanity has made him crazy.
    d) The Lovin Spoonful contributed music to *What's New Pussycat?*

5. The bad guys in *What's Up Tiger Lily?*

    a) Kill
    b) Maim
    c) Call information for numbers they could easily look up themselves
    d) All of the above

6. Woody could have made it twice as funny and half as profitable:

    a) *Casino Royale*
    b) *What's Up Tiger Lily*
    c) *What's New Pussycat*
    d) *The Jim Nabors Show*

7. Match the actor with their character:

    a) Liz Bien   g) Renee
    b) Fitz Fassbinger   h) Sir James Bond
    c) Miss Goodthighs   i) Verner
    d) Michael James   j) Victor
    e) Le Chiffre   k) Carol Werner
    f) "M"

    Woody Allen   Peter OToole
    Ursula Andress   Paula Prentice
    Jacqueline Bisset   Peter Sellers
    Capucine   Romy Schneider
    John Huston   Orson Welles
    David Niven

8. The original Japanese film used in
    What's Up Tiger Lily? was?

    a) Godzilla vs the G-Men
    b) Key of Keys
    c) Sushi Samurai
    d) Yaki Yaki Yaki

9. The villian in *What's Up Tiger Lily?*

    a) Wing Fat   c) Shepard Wong
    b) Phil Moscowitz d) Suky Yaki

10. When Shepard Wong's alarm is triggered
    it plays the following recorded message:

    a) But you don't look Jewish
    b) Hmm, an oriental
    c) Shut the door, I'm naked
    d) This Peter Lorre imitation is killing me

Apprenticeship–
The Early Movies
Answers

1.   a)   Phil Moscowitz

2.   b)   Britt Ekland

3.   b)   *Don't Drink the Water*

4.   a)   True
         b)   True
         c)   True
         d)   False

5.   d)   All of the above

6.   c)   *What's New Pussycat?*

7.   a)   Paula Prentice
           b)   Peter Sellers
           c)   Jacqueline Bisset
           d)   Peter O'Toole
           e)   Orson Welles
           f)   John Huston
           g)   Capucine
           h)   David Niven
           i)   Ursula Andress
           j)   Woody Allen
           k)   Romy Schneider

8.   b)   Key of Keys

9.   a)   Wing Fat

10.   c)   Shut the door, I'm naked

Take the Money and Run
Questions

1. *Take the Money and Run* was distributed by whom?

    a) Orion Pictures
    b) Palomar Pictures
    c) United Artists
    d) The New York *Post* delivery boys

2. Virgil and Louise named their son Jonathan Ralph Starkwell after which of Virgil's relatives?

    a) Brother
    b) Father
    c) Mother
    d) Sister

3.   Who did not appear in *Take the Money and Run*?

    a)   Don Frazier
    b)   Louise Lasser
    c)   Janet Margolin
    d)   Willie Sutton

4.   Virgil's accomplice, Frankie Wolf, was wanted by federal authorities for what crime?

    a)   Bank robbery, assault and getting naked in front of his in-laws
    b)   Arson, robbery, assault with intent to kill and marrying a horse
    c)   Dancing with a mailman
    d)   None of the above

5.   Virgil's grandfather was struck in the head while watching:

    a)   The Brooklyn Dodgers
    b)   The New York Yankees
    c)   The Washington Senators
    d)   His next door neighbors making love to a men's glee club

6.   Match the characters with their professions:

    a)   Bank robber   T.S. Foster
    b)   Cello teacher   William Hummers
    c)   FBI agent   Dorothy Lowry
    d)   Probation officer   Daniel Miller
    e)   Schoolteacher   Mr. Torgman

7.   Who is the narrator in *Take the Money and Run*?

a) Jackson Beck   c) Don Pardo
b) Patrick Horgan   d) Howard Stern

8.   Virgil's former jailmates are now:

a) Priests, rabbis and other blue collar workers
b) Homosexuals, politicians and sports figures
c) Lawyers, insurance salesmen and exotic dancers
d) All of the above

9.   Who was blackmailing Virgil?

a) Miss Blair   c) Mrs. Weinstein
b) Mrs. Cohen   d) Mr. Rogers

10.   Virgil's prison I.D. number was:

a) 29485   c) 36633
b) 34683   d) 6969

11.   What color shirt did Virgil wear to the bank robbery?

a) Beige   c) Pink
b) Blue   d) Plaid

12.   In what manner was Virgil severely disciplined?

a) He was locked in a sweatbox with an insurance salesman.

b) He was sadistically beaten by boys from every religion.
c) He was forced to listen to Wayne Newton records.
d) He was covered with an unpleasant ointment.

13. True or false:

a) Louise was a seamstress.
b) Virgil's uncle has a high speed, electronic, digital computer.
c) The gang attempted to rob the Union Fidelity Bank.
d) Kowalski was a midget.
e) "Real" beauty makes Virgil gag.
f) Virgil was put in a maximum security prison on May 21, 1959.

14. Who produced the boring "short" the bank robbers had to sit through?

a) Steven Spielberg
b) Roger Corman
c) Rollins and Joffe
d) Woody Allen

15. An old roommate knew Virgil wasn't a gynecologist because he didn't:

a) Speak a foreign language
b) Have an accent
c) Rob banks
d) Have a diploma

16. Virgil feels "crime definitely pays" because of which of the following reasons?

   a) The hours are good.
   b) You're your own boss.
   c) You get to meet interesting people.
   d) All of the above.

17. The FBI regarded Virgil as a(n):

   a) Athiest
   b) Pinko
   c) Nuisance
   d) All of the above

18. Convicts on the chain gang were given one hot meal a day. What was it?

   a) Hot cocoa
   b) Chicken from Tresky's
   c) Oatmeal
   d) A bowl of steam

19. Where was Virgil incarcerated?

   a) Attica
   b) Rikers Island
   c) St. Wayne
   d) San Quentin

20. Woody parodies which of the following films?

   a) *City Lights*
   b) *Dark Victory*
   c) *Treasure of Sierra Madre*
   d) *West Side Story*

21.   Who does Virgil's grandfather think he is after
        he's hit on the head with a baseball?

        a) Adolf Hitler
        b) Pope Pius XVI
        c) Joseph Stalin
        d) Kaiser Wilhelm

22.   The prison camp scenes recall those in what
        movie?

        a) *Bridge over the River Kwai*
        b) *Cool Hand Luke*
        c) *The Sand Pebbles*
        d) *White Heat*

23.   Woody pays an obvious hommage to what
        director?

        a) John Ford
        b) John Huston
        c) Fritz Lang
        d) Sam Peckinpah

24.   Virgil does not apply himself "one iota" to his
        cello playing. What would he do?

        a) Blow into it
        b) Peel it
        c) Saw it back and forth with ice tongs
        d) None of the above

Take the Money and Run
Answers

1.   b) Palomar Pictures

2.   c) Mother

3.   d) Willie Sutton

4.   c) Dancing with a mailman

5.   c) The Washington Senators

6.   a) William Hummers
       b) Mr. Torgman
       c) Daniel Miller
       d) T.S. Foster
       e) Dorothy Lowry

7.   a) Jackson Beck

8.   b) Homosexuals, politicians and sports figures

9.   a) Miss Blair

10.   a) 29485

11.   a) Beige

12.   a) He was locked in a sweatbox with an insurance salesman.

13.   a) False   d) False
      b) False   e) True
      c) True   f) True

14.   c) Rollins and Joffe

15.   a) Speak a foreign language

16.   d) All of the above

17.   d) All of the above

18.   d) A bowl of steam

19.   c) St. Wayne

20.   d) *West Side Story*

21.   d) Kaiser Wilhelm

22.   b) *Cool Hand Luke*

23.   c) Fritz Lang

24.   a) Blow into it

Bananas
Questions

1. Who wrote the screenplay for *Bananas*?

    a) Woody Allen
    b) Woody Allen and Marshall Brickman
    c) Woody Allen and Mickey Rose
    d) Marilyn Chambers

2. What was Fielding Mellish's profession?

    a) Bank robber
    b) Film critic
    c) Products tester
    d) Large contributor to the New York City
       Sperm Bank

3. What kind of cake did Fielding bring to dinner?

    a) Apple
    b) Cherry
    c) Prune
    d) None of the above

4.   Who testified against Fielding Mellish?

    a) Miss America
    b) Jimmy "the Weasel" Frattiani
    c) John Dean
    d) Officer O'Reilly

5.   Who did not appear in *Bananas*?

    a) Howard Cosell
    b) Louise Lasser
    c) Janet Margolin
    d) Sylvester Stallone

6.   Fielding Mellish worked for what company?

    a) Executive Fitness Corp.
    b) General Equipment
    c) Progressive Industries
    d) Dick's Vibrator and Sushi Co. Ltd.

7.   True or false:

    a) Dictator Vargas enlisted the help of the UJA.
    b) Fielding purchased *Time, Newsweek, Saturday Review, Commentary* and *Orgasm.*
    c) From now on the citizens of San Marcos will have to change their underwear every half hour.

8.   San Marcos leads the world in:

    a) Banana production
    b) Hernias
    c) Political unrest
    d) Social diseases

9. Fielding loves Eastern philosophy because it's:

    a) Metaphysical
    b) Redundant
    c) Abortively pedantic
    d) All of the above

10. What was the original title of *Bananas*?

    a) *Banana Republic*
    b) *El Weirdo*
    c) *Yes, We Have No Bananas*
    d) None of the above

11. How does Miss America describe Fielding?

    a) A communist
    b) A dirty rat
    c) A spy
    d) A subversive mother

12. At what college is Nancy a student?

    a) Brandeis
    b) City College
    c) Hunter College
    d) NYU

13. According to Nancy, in what way is Fielding immature?

    a) Sexually
    b) Intellectually
    c) Physically
    d) All of the above

14. How many grilled-cheese sandwiches does Fielding order-out?

    a) None
    b) 500
    c) 900
    d) 1000

15. The eating sequence with the rebel girl parodies:

    a) *City Lights*
    b) *Grand Illusion*
    c) *Tom Jones*
    d) *Wild Strawberries*

16. How does Nancy rate Fielding's lovemaking ability?

    a) Great
    b) Lousy
    c) Not the worst I've had
    d) The best I ever had

17. When the rebel leader becomes President the
    national language is changed to:

    a) German
    b) Italian
    c) Spanish
    d) Swedish

18. Fielding is upset at waiting for the revolution
    to take place because:

    a) he's missing his analyst appointments
    b) he parked near his building
    c) he has a rented car
    d) he owes rent

19. Fielding volunteers his services should the rebel
    leader ever need a:

    a) rat
    b) sniffling dog
    c) squirrel
    d) tiger

20. A prisoner is tortured by being forced to listen to:

    a) Caro Nome
    b) Feelings
    c) Naughty Marietta
    d) You Light Up My Life

Bananas
Answers

1. c) Woody Allen and Mickey Rose

2. c) Products tester

3. c) Prune

4. a) Miss America

5. c) Janet Margolin

6. b) General Equipment

7. a) True
    b) True
    c) True

8. b) Hernias

9.   d) All of the above

10.   b) *El Weirdo*

11.   d) A subversive mother

12.   b) City College

13.   d) All of the Above

14.   c) 900

15.   c) *Tom Jones*

16.   c) Not the worst I've had

17.   d) Swedish

18.   c) He has a rented car

19.   c) Squirrel

20.   c) Naughty Marietta

Play It Again, Sam
Questions

1. While getting ready for a blind date, Alan complains, "I shouldn't have used so much _____ under my arms."

    a) Arrid Extra Dry
    b) Binaca
    c) Covousier
    d) Frosted Flakes

2. Who did Alan Felix first date?

    a) Jennifer
    b) Julie
    c) Sharon
    d) Liberace

3.   What is Dick Christy's home phone number?

   a) 873-0972
   b) 621-4598
   c) 726-1245
   d) 764-8150

4.   At what gate is the flight to Cleveland?

   a) 9
   b) 11
   c) 15
   d) 69

5.   What was the Chinese restaurant in *Play It Again, Sam*?

   a) Hong Fat Noodle Company
   b) Large Wong Mandarin
   c) Szechuan Wok
   d) Sid's Bagel Emporium

6.   Match the actress with her character:

   a) Jennifer   Susan Anspach
   b) Julie   Joy Bang
   c) Nancy   Jennifer Salt
   d) Sharon   Viva

7.   In what month does Alan's analyst vacation every year?

   a) April
   b) August
   c) July
   d) June

8.   True or false:

   a) Alan plays Bartok and leaves his Oscar
       Peterson album out.
   b) "How Humphrey Bogart Made Me the
       Superb Lover I Am Today" was the work-
       ing title of *Play It Again, Sam.*
   c) Sandy Keller works for an astrologer.
   d) Linda warned Alan that his date with
       Sharon will be strictly sex.
   e) The rolling hills of San Francisco sym-
       bolize Alan's rising and falling hopes.

9.   If Alan could pick any painting what would he
      pick?

   a) A Monet
   b) A Pollock
   c) A Rembrandt
   d) A Renoir

10.   Alan wanted Linda to tell a blind date that his
      wife died in:

   a) A mine shaft explosion
   b) Bed with a Nazi
   c) Defining protoplasm
   d) A scooter accident

11.   How much did Alan pay for his track medal?

   a) Five bucks
   b) Ten bucks
   c) Fifteen bucks
   d) Twenty bucks

12. What did Alan buy Linda for her birthday?

   a) A watch
   b) A plastic skunk
   c) A negligee
   d) a and c

13. *Play It Again, Sam* was released in:

   a) January 1973
   b) March 1972
   c) May 1972
   d) July 1972

14. When Alan and Linda are laying in bed, a large poster of what Bogart film is seen above them?

   a) Across the Pacific
   b) Casablanca
   c) The Maltese Falcon
   d) Tokyo Joe

15. Linda asks Alan if all he cooks is TV dinners, he replies, "who bothers to cook them,

   a) I don't eat at all
   b) I don't like fried food
   c) I never liked them anyway
   d) I suck them frozen

Play It Again, Sam
Answers

1. b) Binaca

2. c) Sharon

3. b) 621-4598

4. c) 15

5. a) Hong Fat Noodle Company

6. a) Viva   c) Susan Anspach
    b) Joy Bang   d) Jennifer Salt

7. b) August

8. a) True   d) False
    b) False   e) True
    c) True

9.   d)   A Renoir

10.   a)   A mine shaft explosion

11.   d)   Twenty bucks

12.   b)   A plastic skunk

13.   b)   May 1972

14.   a)   Across the Pacific

15.   d)   I suck them frozen

Everything You Always Wanted to Know about Sex... (but were afraid to ask) Questions

1.   Dr. Bernardo was considered mad because he discovered what?

   a) How to make a man impotent by hiding his hat
   b) How to measure the shockwaves emitted by an erection
   c) The principle that penis envy should not be limited to midgets
   d) That sex with barnyard animals is not hazardous to your health
   e) All of the above

2.   Who did not appear in *Everything You Always Wanted to Know*?

   a) Lou Jacobi
   b) Burt Reynolds
   c) Gene Wilder
   d) Tony Roberts

3. Try again!

    a) John Carradine
    b) Tony Randall
    c) Lynn Redgrave
    d) Vanessa Redgrave

4. Dr. Ross was a:

    a) Dentist
    b) General practitioner
    c) Sex therapist
    d) Pervert

5. Which of the following are segments in *Everything You Always Wanted to Know about Sex*?

    a) "What is Perversion?"
    b) "Are Homosexuals Gay?"
    c) "What Happens During Ejaculation?"
    d) "Do Dental Hygienists Enjoy Sex?"

6. Among Dr. Bernardo's experiments are:

    a) A man having intercourse with a loaf of pumpernickel bread
    b) Building a five hundred foot diaphragm
    c) Putting the brain of a lesbian into a man who works for the phone company
    d) Solving the problem of premature ejaculation in elephants

7.   "The Beheading of the Fool" is a parody of:

a) *A Streetcar Named Desire*
b) *Citizen Kane*
c) *Macbeth*
d) *Potemkin*

8.   The breakfast scene in "What is Sodomy"
parodies what film?

a) *A Streetcar Named Desire*
b) *Citizen Kane*
c) *Macbeth*
d) *Potemkin*

9.   Where was Dr. Ross's practice?

a) Brooklyn, NY
b) Jackson Heights, NY
c) Philadelphia, PA
d) Tacoma, WA

10.   What caused Igor's deformity?

a) A four-hour orgasm
b) A lightning bolt
c) What "hump"
d) Poor posture

11.   True or false: Woody played the following
characters.

a) Antonio
b) Dr. Ross
c) Fool
d) Sperm

12.   The scene with the Fool and his
        father parodies:

        a)   Hamlet
        b)   La Strada
        c)   MacBeth
        d)   The Seventh Seal

13.   Comme un salmon fredoo is translated into:

        a)   Are you small?
        b)   Go easy on my hymen.
        c)   Now take your pants off.
        d)   You just lay there passive – like a lox.

14.   Woody (as a sperm cell) has which of the
        following anxieties?

        a)   He's worrying about slamming his head
             against hard rubber.
        b)   If it's going to be a homosexual
             encounter?
        c)   If the guy is masturbating, he'll wind up
             on the ceiling.
        d)   All of the above.

15.   The rabbi's fantasy on What's My
        Perversion was:

        a)   Being whipped while his wife ate pork.
        b)   Exposing himself on subways.
        c)   Stroking rosary beads with matzos.
        d)   Waving his private parts at the audience.

Everything You Always Wanted to Know about Sex... (but were afraid to ask) Answers

1.   a) How to make a man impotent by hiding his hat

2.   d) Tony Roberts

3.   d) Vanessa Redgrave

4.   b) General Practitioner

5.   c) "What Happens during Ejaculation?"

6.   c) Putting the brain of a lesbian into a man who works for the phone company

7.   c) *Macbeth*

8.   b) *Citizen Kane*

9.   b) Jackson Heights, NY

10.   a) A four-hour orgasm

11.   a) True
       b) False
       c) True
       d) True

12.   a) *Hamlet*

13.   d) You just lay there, like a lox.

14.   d) All of the above.

15.   a) Being whipped while his wife ate pork.

Sleeper
Questions

1.   In what locale was most of *Sleeper* filmed?

   a) California
   b) Colorado
   c) New York
   d) San Francisco

2.   Woody stayed in the same bungalow that Clark
      Gable used during the filming of what movie?

   a) *Gone with the Wind*
   b) *It Happened One Night*
   c) *Possessed*
   d) *San Francisco*

3. According to Miles, there's intelligence to the universe—except for certain parts of:

   a) City Hall
   b) New Jersey
   c) Queens
   d) Washington, D.C.

4. Miles was the owner of what?

   a) A clothing store
   b) A health food store
   c) A women's lingerie store
   d) None of the above

5. Miles once took a political stand by:

   a) Not voting
   b) Not eating grapes for twenty-four hours
   c) Not selling yogurt for a week
   d) Putting oats on his head

6. The breakfast scene was a parody of:

   a) *Along the Waterfront*
   b) *Citizen Kane*
   c) *Key Largo*
   d) *Shanghai Express*

7. The robot tailors in *Sleeper* were:

   a) Aloisi and Butler
   b) Ginsberg and Cohen
   c) Rodriguez and Weinstein
   d) Shlein and R2D2

8. What is Miles Monroe's dog's name?

   a) King
   b) Rags
   c) Reds
   d) Spot

9. True or false—When Miles is asked to identify relics from two hundred years ago he states
   that:

   a) Charles DeGaulle was a famous French
      chef.
   b) Howard Cosell was an ear, nose and mouth
      specialist.
   c) Marlon Brando was the founder of Weight
      Watchers.
   d) Bela Lugosi was once the mayor of New
      York.
   e) Abbie Hoffman once chanted the word
      "pudding" until his demands were met.

10. *Sleeper* received an Academy Award nomina-
    tion for:

    a) Best Costume Design
    b) Best Director
    c) Best Screenplay
    d) Received no Academy Award nomination

11. How much was the Preservation Jazz Hall Band
    paid for their work on the *Sleeper* soundtrack?

    a) Nothing
    b) $12,000
    c) $20,000
    d) $35,000

12. What was Luna's last name?

   a) Rago
   b) Saragnese
   c) Schlosser
   d) Weintraub

13. In the year 2173 all men are impotent except those of what descent?

   a) Armenian
   b) Italian
   c) Jewish
   d) Mongolian

14. Who was the leader of the "underground movement"?

   a) Emo
   b) Erno
   c) Groucho
   d) Harpo

15. Who won the beauty contest?

   a) Miss California
   b) Miss Florida
   c) Miss Hawaii
   d) Miss Montana

16. Who was the Trotskyite who became a Jesus freak and was arrested for selling pornography connect-the-dots books?

   a) Vivian Gornick
   b) Lisa Sorenson
   c) Vicky Tiel
   d) Susan Winter

17. According to Miles, what's it like being dead for two hundred years?

a) Living in Queens
b) Watching a game show
c) Spending a weekend in Beverly Hills
d) None of the above

18. Miles dangling on computer tape on the side of a skyscraper is reminiscent of:

a) Fatty Arbuckle
b) Charlie Chaplin
c) Buster Keaton
d) Harold Lloyd

19. Who once beat up Miles?

a) His doorman
b) Quakers
c) Albert Shanker
d) Sister Mary Theresa

20. For what type of operation did Miles go into the hospital?

a) Brain
b) Hernia
c) Hysterectomy
d) Ulcer

21. Miles told Luna that he was once a lifeguard at:

a) Atlantic City
b) Bloomingdale's
c) Coney Island
d) Venice Beach

22. What course did Luna take at the University?

   a) Cosmetic Sexual Technique and Poetry
   b) Oral Satisfaction and Dental Hygiene
   c) Petting and Hotel Management
   d) Zipper removal and pruning

23. Miles was afraid he'd see something "weird and futuristic" like:

   a) the body of a crab with the head of a social worker.
   b) the face of a fish with the voice of Rona Barrett.
   c) the head of a city official with the brains of an imbecile.
   d) none of the above.

24. What was not taken into consideration when deciding whether or not to clone?

   a) Cloning hadn't been perfected
   b) Erno wasn't there
   c) The Pinnochio Factor
   d) There was no sterile surgical equipment

25. How long has it been since Miles has had sex?

   a) 200 years
   b) 204 years (if you count his marriage)
   c) He's never had sex
   d) All of the above

Sleeper
Answers

1.   b)   Colorado

2.   b)   *It Happened One Night*

3.   b)   New Jersey

4.   b)   A health food store

5.   b)   Not eating grapes for twenty-four hours

6.   b)   *Citizen Kane*

7.   b)   Ginsberg and Cohen

8.   b)   Rags

9. a) True   c) False   e) False
    b) False   d) True

10. d) Received no Academy Award nomination

11. b) $12,000

12. c) Schlosser

13. b) Italian

14. b) Erno

15. d) Miss Montana

16. b) Lisa Sorenson

17. c) Spending a weekend in Beverly Hills

18. d) Harold Lloyd

19. b) Quakers

20. b) Hernia

21. b) Bloomingdale's

22. a) Cosmetic Sexual Technique and Poetry

23. a) The body of a crab with the head of a social worker

24. The Pinocchio Factor

25. b) 204 years (if you count his marriage)

Love and Death
Questions

1. According to Woody, which of the following comedians would have been ideal for his character in *Love and Death*?

    a) Charlie Chaplin
    b) Bob Hope
    c) Groucho Marx
    d) Ronald Reagan

2. Why does Boris think Napoleon has invaded Austria?

    a) He was out of Cognac.
    b) He ran out of Courvoisier.
    c) He wanted to meet the Pope.
    d) He was incredibly horny.

3.   The Village Idiot convention was held in:

   a) Dallas
   b) Minsk
   c) Moscow
   d) Washington, D.C.

4.   The music in *Love and Death* was composed
     by:

   a) Mozart
   b) Prokofiev
   c) Stravinsky
   d) Wagner

5.   In which location was *Love and Death* primarily
     filmed?

   a) Budapest
   b) Paris
   c) Upstate New York
   d) Warsaw

6.   Boris contemplated committing suicide by what
     means?

   a) Eating unleavened borscht
   b) Inhaling next to an Armenian
   c) Masturbating to the French national anthem
   d) Shooting himself

7.   Some men are heterosexual and some men are
     homosexual and some men never think of sex
     and they become:

   a) Catholics
   b) Lawyers
   c) Street vendors
   d) Telephone operators

8. There are worse things than death—like spending an evening with:

   a) An insurance salesman
   b) The editor of *Astrology Monthly*
   c) The infield of the Philadelphia Phillies
   d) Your mother-in-law

9. Uncle Nicolai:

   a) Hit Boris with a pig bladder
   b) Learned the lyrics to "Rag Mop"
   c) Owns a pelican
   d) Was repulsive

10. True or false:

    a) Sonia describes herself as half saint/half whore.
    b) Young Gregor is older than Old Gregor.
    c) Stravinsky music was considered too powerful for *Love and Death*.
    d) Mikhail and Raskov are Boris's brothers.
    e) Voskevec went to bed with a herring.

11. What was the budget for *Love and Death*?

    a) $1,000,000
    b) $2,000,000
    c) $3,500,000
    d) $5,000,000

12. The Village Idiot is happy because his one concern in life is:

    a) Figuring out how much saliva to dribble
    b) Saving string
    c) Stroking a little piece of velvet
    d) None of the above

13.   Boris's search for a sign of God's existence parallels:

a) *8½*
b) *La Strada*
c) *Persona*
d) *The Seventh Seal*

14.   The blending of Sonia and Natasha's faces echoes Bergman's:

a) *Fanny and Alexander*
b) *Persona*
c) *The Seventh Seal*
d) *Wild Strawberries*

15.   The only difference between Napoleon and the czar is that:

a) Napoleon is wealthier.
b) The czar is a little taller.
c) Napoleon likes to recite his credits.
d) The czar can fix fences.

16.   On the development of what food did the balance of Europe depend?

a) Beef Wellington
b) Blintzes
c) Napoleons
d) Veal Francisco

17.   How was brother Ivan killed?

a) Contracted a social disease
b) Stabbed to death by a Polish conscientious objector
c) Stampeded by sheep
d) None of the above

18.   What condiment does Boris offer to bring to bed?

   a) Catsup
   b) Mustard
   c) Soy sauce
   d) Tartar sauce

19.   While dangling at the end of a rope, Boris had a sudden desire to live. What did he want to do?

   a) Hold Sonia close to him
   b) Weep tears on her shoulder
   c) Engage in oral sex
   d) All of the above

20.   What is the French title of *Love and Death*?

21.   The general's view of the soldiers parallels:

   a) Bergman's *The Seventh Seal*
   b) Chaplin's *Modern Times*
   c) Eisenstein's *Alexander Nevsky*
   d) Lang's *You Only Live Once*

22.   Boris finds his snow steak:

   a) Delicious
   b) Overdone
   c) Rare
   d) Undercooked

23.   What's Boris's "favorite pastime"?

   a) Awaiting his execution
   b) Collecting butterflies
   c) Making love
   d) None of the above

24. "Death," who appears and dances off with Boris resembles a similar scene in which Ingmar Bergman film?

25. Among the many problems that the wicked man will incur are:

a) His tongue shall cleave to the roof of his mouth.
b) He shall speak like a woman.
c) He shall be delivered to his enemy, whether they can pay the delivery charge or not.
d) All of the above.

Love and Death
Answers

1.   b)   Bob Hope

2.   b)   He ran out of Courvoisier.

3.   b)   Minsk

4.   b)   Prokofiev

5.   a)   Budapest

6.   b)   Inhaling next to an Armenian

7.   b)   Lawyers

8.   a)   An insurance salesman

9.   d)   Was repulsive

10. a) True   d) True
     b) True   e) True
     c) True

11. b) 2,000,000

12. a) Figuring out how much saliva to dribble

13. d) *The Seventh Seal*

14. b) *Persona*

15. b) The czar is a little taller.

16. c) Napoleons

17. b) Stabbed to death by a Polish conscientious objector

18. c) Soy sauce

19. d) All of the above

20. Guerre et Amour

21. b) Chaplin's *Modern Times*

22. c) Rare

23. a) Awaiting his execution

24. *The Seventh Seal*

25. d) All of the above

The Front
Questions

1.   Who directed *The Front*?

   a)   Woody Allen
   b)   Sam Peckinpah
   c)   Martin Ritt
   d)   Richard Nixon

2.   Who does not appear in *The Front*?

   a)   Herschel Bernardi
   b)   Michael Murphy
   c)   Zero Mostel
   d)   Joseph Stalin

3.   In what city was *The Front* filmed?

   a)   Los Angeles
   b)   Manhattan
   c)   San Francisco
   d)   Moscow

4. Match the actor with the year he was blacklisted:

   a) Herschel Bernardi   1950
   b) Walter Bernstein   1951
   c) Martin Ritt   1952
   d) Joshua Shelley   1953

5. What was the name of the television show to which Howard "fronted" scripts?

   a) "Citizen's on Parade"
   b) "Commonwealth Theater"
   c) "Ford Family Hour"
   d) "Grand Central"

6. True or false:

   a) The scene in which Hecky Brown received an embarrassing $250 as a headline performer actually happened to Zero Mostel.
   b) Hecky's suicide was based on real-life TV actor Philip Loeb.
   c) The biggest sin in the Prince family is to pay retail.
   d) *The Front* was Andrea Marcovicci's first major film appearance.

7. Who does not appear in *The Front*?

   a) Danny Aiello
   b) John Doumanian
   c) Michael Murphy
   d) Jack Slater

8.   Florence falls in love with the image that Howard projects. In what other film does the feminine lead do the same?

    a) *Bananas*
    b) *Play It Again, Sam*
    c) *Love and Death*
    d) *September*

9.   When asked if he knew Al Miller, Howard's response was:

    a) How you do mean?, in the Biblical sense?
    b) no
    c) who
    d) yes

10.   When a sponsor remarks that some of the actors look pretty pink, Howard replies:

    a) It's just the make-up
    b) Later they'll turn blue
    c) The lighting is just bad
    d) None of the above

The Front
Answers

1.   c) Martin Ritt

2.   d) Joseph Stalin

3.   b) Manhattan

4.   a) 1953   c) 1951
        b) 1950   d) 1952

5.   d) "Grand Central"

6.   a) True   c) True
        b) True   d) True

7.   b) John Doumanian

8.   a) *Bananas*

9.   a) In the Biblical sense

10.   a) It's just the make-up

Annie Hall
Questions

1.   Who did not appear in *Annie Hall*?

   a) Shelley Duvall
   b) Franz Kafka
   c) Tony Roberts
   d) Paul Simon

2.   Try again!

   a) Colleen Dewhurst
   b) Carol Kane
   c) Geraldine Page
   d) Sigourney Weaver

3.   One more time!!

   a) Jeff Goldblum
   b) Shelley Hack
   c) Michael Murphy
   d) Christopher Walken

4. Who was Alvy's first wife?

   a) Allison
   b) Harlene
   c) Robin
   d) Bruce

5. What was *Annie Hall* almost titled?

   a) *Anhedonia*
   b) *A Rollercoaster Named Desire*
   c) *It Had to Be a Jew*
   d) All of the above

6. Alvy is going to give his analyst one more year and then he's going:

   a) To get a lobotomy
   b) To go to Lourdes
   c) To get a brain transplant
   d) To stop eating pork

7. How long has Alvy been killing spiders?

   a) Since he was thirty
   b) Since he's been taking tennis lessons
   c) Since he became a vegetarian
   d) Since he took EST

8. What does Alvy consider a notch below child molesters?

   a) Autograph seekers
   b) Insurance salesmen
   c) Politicians
   d) TV game show hosts

9. What was the first book Alvy bought for Annie?

    a) *Death in Venice*
    b) *Denial of Death*
    c) *The Cat Book*
    d) *The Joy of Sex*

10. "She" was such a lively dancer. Who was she?

    a) Aunt Natalie
    b) Aunt Sarah
    c) Aunt Tessie
    d) Bobby Burgess

11. According to Alvy, life is divided into two categories. What are they?

    a) The bad and the worse
    b) The moral and the immoral
    c) The horrible and the miserable
    d) The rotten and the terrible

12. True or false:

    a) Scenes dealing with Alvy's childhood were artificially colored yellow.
    b) Classmate Donald used to be a heroin addict; now he's a methadone addict.
    c) The coke fiend was played by John Doumanian.
    d) *Annie Hall* won the Director's Guild Award.
    e) The classroom scene in *Annie Hall* was derived from Fellini's *8½*.
    f) *Annie Hall* won four Academy Awards.

13. *Annie Hall* was originally about:

a) Life in Manhattan
b) Obsessive sexual behavior
c) Woody exclusively
d) A fantasy about the ideal woman

14. Alvy is making excellent progress in analysis. Pretty soon:

a) He won't have to lie down on the couch.
b) He won't have to wear the lobster bib.
c) He won't have to be coaxed out of the hamper.
d) He'll be able to take off the pinwheel hat.

15. What happened the last time Alvy took a puff at a party?

a) He had a dream that a woodchuck was trying to claim his prize at the raffle.
b) He tried to take his pants off over his head.
c) He was only able to grow one sideburn.
d) He broke his teeth giving the Statue of Liberty a hickey.

16. To which hotel did Tony Lacy invite Alvy and Annie for drinks?

a) Doral Hotel
b) Edison Hotel
c) Pierre Hotel
d) Plaza Hotel

17.   Which person would call Alvy ''a real Jew''?

   a)   Annie's mother
   b)   Grammy Hall
   c)   Dwayne
   d)   Father

18.   What song can be heard during Alvy's closing monologue?

   a)   ''A Hard Way to Go''
   b)   ''It Had to Be You''
   c)   ''Seems Like Old Times''
   d)   b and c

19.   Who is the person who always bothered Alvy as a youth?

   a)   Aunt Tessie
   b)   Max
   c)   Joey Nichols
   d)   Alvy's father

20.   Who muttered ''Jew'' under his breath?

   a)   Max
   b)   Tom Christie
   c)   The guys from NBC
   d)   None of the above

21.   When Max puts a grotesque sun visor over his head, Alvy wants to know if:

   a)   They're going to the TV show.
   b)   They're driving through plutonium.
   c)   They still have time to meet Annie.
   d)   He's going to Tony Lacy's party.

22. What "conspiracy" theory does Alvy use to avoid having sex with Allison?

    a) Bay of Pigs
    b) Kennedy Assassination
    c) The Warren Report
    d) None of the above

23. What disease did George have?

    a) Agoraphobia
    b) Epilepsy
    c) Meningitis
    d) Narcolepsy

24. From what Disney movie do we see an animated scene?

    a) *Cinderella*
    b) *Fantasia*
    c) *Sleeping Beauty*
    d) *Snow White*

25. After making love to Annie, Alvy exults:

    a) "As Balzac said, 'There goes another novel.' "
    b) "I'll never play the piano again."
    c) "That was the most fun I ever had without laughing."
    d) All of the above

26. Alvy can't get with any religion that advertises where?

    a) *Playboy*
    b) *Popular Mechanics*
    c) *The Christian Science Monitor*
    d) The Port Authority

27. The doctor who treats Alvy's anxiety attack in California has a striking resemblance to whom?

a) William F. Buckley
b) Dr. Flicker
c) Joey Nichols
d) Jack Rollins

28. Alvy jokes about dating a woman from what administration?

a) Eisenhower
b) Johnson
c) Nixon
d) Roosevelt

29. The Halls and the Singers are like:

a) Laurel and Hardy
b) Leopold and Loeb
c) Oil and water
d) Sacco and Vanzetti

30. The spider in Annie's bathroom was the size of a what?

a) Beaver
b) Buick
c) Social worker
d) Winnebago

31. When Annie dated in high school, she probably looked:

a) Like the wife of an astronaut
b) Neat
c) Pretty
d) Silly

32. Who was Alvy's second wife?

   a) Allison
   b) Annie
   c) Robin
   d) Susan

33. Who has a chair in philosophy at Cornell?

   a) Henry Drucker
   b) Paul Goodman
   c) Herschel Kaminsky
   d) Douglas Wyeth

34. Which of the following scenes was cut from *Annie Hall*?

   a) In the pink there, Mr. Miami Beach
   b) Look at Mr. Slick. He has a charge account at Gucci's
   c) The winner of the Truman Capote lookalike contest
   d) These guys are back from Fire Island...they're sort of giving it a chance.

35. What course did Annie take at school?

   a) *Beowoulf*
   b) Introduction to the Novel
   c) Contemporary Crisis in Western Man
   d) Existential Motifs in Russian Literature

36. Alvy hasn't been the same since he quit smoking. How long has it been?

   a) Two weeks
   b) Six months
   c) Sixteen years
   d) He never smoked

37. The annoying guy on the movie line probably ran an ad for a woman who likes James Joyce, Mozart and:

    a) Anatomy
    b) Marshall McLuhan
    c) Pudding
    d) Sodomy

38. Who did cocaine and were a "lot of laughs"?

    a) Armenian women
    b) Dallas Cowboys
    c) Incas
    d) Persians

39. Alvy was a great schoolyard athlete. Once Max threw him a football once and he what?

    a) Ate it
    b) Dribbled it
    c) Kicked it
    d) Swallowed it

40. Tony Lacy's house was owned by each of the following except:

    a) Charlie Chaplin
    b) Legs Diamond
    c) Nelson Eddy
    d) Douglas Fairbanks

41. What did Alvy think they gave out for Tony Lacy's music?

    a) Awards
    b) Earplugs
    c) Grammies
    d) Suppositories

42.   Alvy's father did what kind of work?

   a)   Caddy at a miniature golf course
   b)   Manager at an amusement park
   c)   Ran a bumper car concession
   d)   None of the above

43.   "Everything our parents said was good for us
       is back; sun, milk, red meat—and what else?

   a)   Apples
   b)   College
   c)   Relationships
   d)   Tennis

44.   At what theatre did Annie and Alvy see *The
       Sorrow and the Pity*?

   a)   Cinema Village
   b)   Thalia
   c)   The Beekman
   d)   The New Yorker

45.   Why didn't Alvy shower at the tennis club?

   a)   He never showers in a public place.
   b)   He doesn't like to get naked in front of
        another man.
   c)   He doesn't like to show his body to a man
        of his gender.
   d)   All of the above

46.   In a scene that was cut from *Annie Hall*, there
       was a discussion of the afterlife during which
       a street elevator rose from the ground bearing

the Devil. The Devil then conducted a tour of Hell's nine layers. What is found on layer five?

a) Insurance salesmen, lawyers and people who dribble
b) Organized crime, fascists dictators and people who don't appreciate oral sex
c) TV executives, clerks from the MTA and people who talk too loudly in movie lines
d) The KKK, ex-wives and people who shine your shoes against your will

47. To what movie did Annie and Alvy arrive late?

a) *Cries and Whispers*
b) *Face to Face*
c) *The Sorrow and the Pity*
d) *Triumph of the Will*

48. To what theater was Annie dragging her new boyfriend to see *The Sorrow and the Pity*?

a) The Beekman
b) Cinema Village
c) The Thalia
d) Theatre 80

49. Who was in the choir with Annie?

50. Alvy was depressed as a child because:

a) He lived in Brooklyn.
b) He had too much hostility.
c) His analyst was a Freudian.
d) The universe is expanding.

Annie Hall
Answers

1.   b)   Franz Kafka

2.   c)   Geraldine Page

3.   c)   Michael Murphy

4.   a)   Allison

5.   d)   All of the above

6.   b)   To go to Lourdes

7.   a)   Since he was thirty

8.   c)   Politicians

9.   b)   *Denial of Death*

Annie Hall—Answers

10. c) Aunt Tessie

11. c) The horrible and the miserable

12. a) True   d) True
    b) True   e) True
    c) True   f) True

13. c) Woody exclusively

14. b) He won't have to wear the lobster bib.

15. b) He tried to take his pants off over his head.

16. c) Pierre Hotel

17. b) Grammy Hall

18. c) "Seems Like Old Times"

19. c) Joey Nichols

20. b) Tom Christie

21. b) They're driving through plutonium.

22. b) Kennedy Assassination

23. d) Narcolepsy

24. a) *Cinderella*

25. d) All of the above

26.   b)   *Popular Mechanics*

27.   b)   Dr. Flicker

28.   a)   Eisenhower

29.   c)   Oil and water

30.   b)   Buick

31.   a)   Like the wife of an astronaut

32.   c)   Robin

33.   c)   Herschel Kaminsky

34.   b)   Look at Mr. Slick. He has a charge account at Gucci's.

35.   d)   Existential Motifs in Russian Literature

36.   c)   Sixteen years

37.   d)   Sodomy

38.   c)   Incas

39.   b)   Dribbled it

40.   d)   Douglas Fairbanks

41.   b)   Earplugs

42.   c)   Ran a bumper car concession

43. b) College

44. d) The *New Yorker*

45. d) All of the above

46. b) Organized crime, fascist dictators and people who don't appreciate oral sex

47. b) *Face to Face*

48. c) The Thalia

49. Randolph Hunt

50. d) The universe is expanding.

Interiors
Questions

1. True or false—Interiors received Academy Award nominations for:

   a) Geraldine Page—Best Actress
   b) Maureen Stapleton—Best Supporting Actress
   c) Kristin Griffith—Best Supporting Actress
   d) Diane Keaton—Best Supporting Actress
   e) E.G. Marshall—Best Actor
   f) Best Director
   g) Best Picture
   h) Best Screenplay
   i) Art Direction

2. Who saved Joey with mouth-to-mouth resuscitation?

   a) Flyn
   b) Mike
   c) Renata
   d) Pearl

105

3. Whose tears at her mother's funeral was an abondonment of her image?

   a) Flyn
   b) Joey
   c) Renata
   d) Pearl

4. Ture or false:

   a) The British monthly, *Films and Filming* named *Interiors* the best film from any source in 1978.
   b) Renata was a successful novelist.
   c) Like Eve, Joey is an interior decorator.

5. She was very high strung, a bright kid; she was sensitive...

   a) Eve
   b) Flyn
   c) Joey
   d) Renata

Interiors
Answers

1. a) True   d) False   g) True
    b) True   e) True   h) True
    c) False   f) False   i) False

2. c) Pearl

3. a) Flyn

4. a) True
    b) False
    c) False

5. c) Joey

Manhattan Questions

1.   True or false:

   a)   Mariel Hemingway received an Academy Award nomination for her role in *Manhattan*.
   b)   Mary Wilke's ex-husband was Jeremiah.
   c)   Tracy was going to Parris for a year.
   d)   Isaac and Tracy went to John's Pizza in the Village.
   e)   Andrew Sarris called *Manhattan* the only truly great movie of the seventies.
   f)   Isaac and Willi picked up two girls at the Russian Tea Room.

2.   "Waffles" is a:

   a)   Diane Arbus subject
   b)   Dachshund
   c)   One-act play
   d)   Isaac's favorite breakfast

3.   Who did not appear in *Manhattan*?

   a)   Anne Byrne
   b)   Karen Ludwig
   c)   Michael Murphy
   d)   Tony Roberts

4.   Who was Isaac's first wife?

   a)   Jill
   b)   Tina
   c)   Vicky
   d)   Melvin

5.   Isaac's second ex-wife published a book called:

   a)   *Freedom at Last*
   b)   *Marriage, Divorce and Selfhood*
   c)   *The Romantic Lesbian Guide*
   d)   *War and Piece*

6.   Tracy attended what school?

   a)   Dalton School
   b)   Julliard
   c)   NYU
   d)   School of Visual Arts

7.   Yale and Mary's Academy of the Overrated include:

   a)   Bergman, Mahler and Boll
   b)   Fitzgerald, Bach and Mailer
   c)   Van Gogh, Fellini and Bruce
   d)   All of the above

8. The list of things that Isaac thought made life
    worth living included:

    a) Kafka, Central Park and Louis Armstrong
    b) Willie Mays, the Seven Beauties and Potato
       Head Blues
    c) Eating chutney, grinning at Persians and
       rooting for the NY Knicks
    d) The crabs at Sam Wo's, Groucho Marx and
       the apples and pears by Cezanne

9. What was the title of the short story Isaac wrote
    about his mother?

    a) "The Castrating Zionist"
    b) "The Seven Year Bitch"
    c) "The Catatonic Nazi"
    d) "Unable to Survive One Mother"

10. Who was the winner of the Zelda Fitzgerald
    Emotional Maturity Award?

    a) Emily
    b) Mary
    c) Tracy
    d) Little Richard

11. Isaac's first wife, Tina, went from teaching
    kindergarten to:

    a) Homosexuality—primal scream—the Mor-
       mons' Washington Post
    b) Drugs—EST—Moonies—William Morris
       Agency
    c) Prostitution—hypnotherapy—Catholism—
       Prudential Insurance Co.
    d) None of the above

12. Who is Mary's analyst?

a) Dr. Chomsky
b) Donnie
c) Max
d) Sigmund

13. Match the scene with the songs:

a) Mary and Isaac driving to the country
b) Isaac and Mary dancing
c) Willie and Isaac's football game
d) Mary and Isaac at the MOMA
e) Tracy leaving for London
f) Carriage ride through Central Park

"He Loves and She Loves"
"Let's Call the Whole Thing Off"
"Embraceable You"
"'S Wonderful"
"Love Is Sweeping"
"They're Writing Songs of Love, but Not for Me"

14. Yale compromises in which of the following ways:

a) betraying his friendship with Isaac
b) neglecting his book
c) denying his wife's desire for children
d) all of the above

15. Yale considers it the "new pornography"

a) divorce
b) gossip
c) tearing down old buildings
d) wheel of fortune

16.   *Manhattan's* depiction of decaying culture is a homage to what movie?

    a) *8½*
    b) *Grand Illusion*
    c) *Potemkin*
    d) *The Seventh Seal*

17.   At what restaurant did Mary and Yale break-up?

    a) Stanhope Cafe
    b) Tavern on the Green
    c) Yellowfingers
    d) Times Square Cafe

18.   Tracy and Isaac shop at:

    a) Dean and Deluca's Food Shop
    b) Juliano's
    c) Smiler's
    d) The Brooklyn Hair and Cheese Emporium

19.   Isaac and Tracy meet Mary and Yale at which museum?

    a) Guggenheim Museum
    b) Jewish Museum
    c) MOMA
    d) Whitney Museum

20.   Isaac wrote for what TV show?

    a) "Fernwood Tonight"
    b) "Human Beings-Wow!"
    c) "Mary Hartman"
    d) None of the above

Manhattan
Answers

1.   a) True   d) True
           b) True   e) True
           c) False   f) False

2.   b) Dachshund

3.   d) Tony Roberts

4.   b) Tina

5.   b) *Marriage, Divorce and Selfhood*

6.   a) Dalton School

7.   a) Bergman, Mahler and Boll

8.   d) The crabs at Sam Wo's, Groucho Marx and the apples and pears by Cézanne

9.   a) "The Castrating Zionist"

10. b) Mary

11. b) Drugs—EST—Moonies—William Morris Agency

12. b) Donnie

13. a) "'S Wonderful"
     b) "Embraceable You"
     c) "Love is Sweeping
     d) "Let's Call the Whole Thing Off"
     e) "They're Writing Songs of Love, But Not for Me"
     f) "He Loves and She Loves"

14. d) All of the above

15. b) Gossip

16. b) *Grand Illusion*

17. a) Stanhope Cafe

18. a) Dean and Deluca's Food Shoop

19. a) Guggenheim Museum

20. b) Human Beings—Wow!

Stardust Memories
Questions

1. Match the actress with her character

   a) Marie Christine Barrault   Daisy
   b) Jessica Harper   Dorrie
   c) Charlotte Rampling   Isobel

2. Jack Rollins appears as a studio executive in *Stardust Memories*. In what other film does he appear?

   a) *Annie Hall*
   b) *Broadway Danny Rose*
   c) *Hannah and Her Sisters*
   d) *September*

3. For what would Sandy trade in his Oscar?

   a) A date with a *Playboy* centerfold
   b) Ten minutes of peace and quiet
   c) One more second of life
   d) The opportunity of quietly humping his analyst

117

4.　　Who identifies himself or herself as trouble?

a) Daisy
b) Dorrie
c) Isobel
d) Sandy

5.　　How can Sandy Bates help the world?

a) Sharing his humor
b) Being more positive
c) Contributing to more charities
d) Telling funnier jokes

6.　　When Sandy is caught in traffic he asks if the Pope or some other _____ is in town.

a) Clown
b) Communist
c) Gestapo
d) Showbiz figure

7.　　With what Greek god does Sandy identify?

a) Jupiter
b) Narcissus
c) Thor
d) Zeus

8.　　Sidney Finkelstein's hostility killed whom?

a) His teacher
b) His ex-wife
c) Her alimony lawyer
d) All of the above

9. What movie do Sandy and Daisy see?

   a) *La Strada*
   b) *Persona*
   c) *The Bicycle Thief*
   d) *Wild Strawberries*

10. What is the name of the restaurant where Sandy brings Isobel and her children for ice cream?

    a) The Pelican Diner
    b) Frank's Restaurant
    c) Carvel
    d) Kingfish Restaurant

11. Robert Munk's (Sandy as a boy) brother Jonathan appears as the Woody child character in what movie?

    a) *Annie Hall*
    b) *Love and Death*
    c) *Radio Days*
    d) *Take the Money and Run*

12. _____ did a definitive cinematic study of (13) _____ Marx.

    a) Chico
    b) Dorrie
    c) Groucho
    d) Harpo
    e) Libby
    f) Sandy
    g) Zeppo

13.   What song plays in the background as Sandy recalls that "perfect" moment?

    a) "Moonlight Serenade"
    b) "Paper Doll"
    c) "Stardust"
    d) "When Will I Be Loved?"

14.   What song plays in the background as Sandy recalls that "perfect" moment?

    a) Moonlight Serenade
    b) Paper Doll
    c) Stardust
    d) When Will I be Loved

15.   What was the studio's setting for Jazz Heaven?

    a) a garbage dump
    b) Frank's Restarant
    c) the Stardust Hotel
    d) the train station

Stardust Memories
Answers

1.   a)   Isobel
       b)   Daisy
       c)   Dorrie

2.   b)   *Broadway Danny Rose*

3.   c)   One more second of life

4.   b)   Dorrie

5.   d)   Telling funnier jokes

6.   d)   Showbiz figure

7.   d)   Zeus

8.   d)   All of the above

9.   c)   *The Bicycle Thief*

10.   b)   *Frank's Restaurant*

11.   b)   *Love and Death*

12.   e)   Libby

13.   f)   Zeppo

14.   c)   Stardust

15.   c)   The Stardust Hotel

A Midsummer's Night
Sex Comedy
Questions

1.   Who wears Blue Moonglow?

    a) Ariel
    b) Adrian
    c) Dulcy
    d) Truman Capote

2.   Andrew made love to Ariel:

    a) Never
    b) Once
    c) Several times
    d) While reading an instruction manual

3.   The music in *A Midsummer's Night Sex Comedy* was by:

    a) Beethoven
    b) Mendelssohn
    c) Prokofiev
    d) Vivaldi

4.   Which of the following did Andrew say?

   a) "Sex alleviates tension, love causes it."
   b) "I help people with their investments un-
      til they don't have any money left."
   c) "Marriage is the death of hope."
   d) a and b
   e) All of the above

5.   Who said, "The saddest thing in the world is
       a missed opportunity"?

   a) Andrew
   b) Leopold
   c) Maxwell
   d) Jim Bakker

6.   Match the characters and their last name:

   a) Ariel   Ford
   b) Dulcy   Jordan
   c) Leopold   Sturgis
   d) Maxwell   Weymouth

7.   Who wears Bay Rum?

   a) Andrew
   b) Leopold
   c) Maxwell
   d) Tommy Tune

   True or false

8.   Because of his problems in bed
       Andrew can now fly.

9.   Dulcy "lost it" in a hammock.

10.   The film takes place circa 1906.

A Midsummer's Night
Sex Comedy
Answers

1. a) Ariel

2. b) Once

3. b) Mendelssohn

4. d) a and b

5. a) Andrew

6. a) Weymouth
    b) Ford
    c) Sturgis
    d) Jordan

7. c) Maxwell

8. True

9. True

10. True

Broadway Danny Rose
Questions

1. The comedic roundtable in *Broadway Danny Rose* included whom?

   a) Sandy Baron, Herb Schlein and Jackie Mason
   b) Jack Rollins, Jackie Gayle and Corbett Monica
   c) Danny Rose, Lou Canova and Milton Berle
   d) Moe, Larry and Curly

2. Danny Rose had a bad year; if things don't pick up he'll:

   a) Commit suicide
   b) Have to sell aluminum siding
   c) Have to start working the Catskills again
   d) Have to sell storm windows

127

3. Match the saying with the philosopher:

   a) Acceptance, forgiveness and love
   b) You can't ride two horses with one behind
   c) If you hate yourself, you hate your work
   d) Friendly, but not familiar

   Aunt Rose   Uncle Morris
   Danny's father   Uncle Sidney

4. Carmine Vitale was wrong about what?

   a) Barney Dunn being the beard
   b) Being shot in the back
   c) Danny Rose being Tina's lover
   d) Who shot J.R.

5. What is the restaurant featured in *Broadway Danny Rose*?

   a) Carnegie delie
   b) Elaine's
   c) John's
   d) The Saloon

6. Who does not appear in *Broadway Danny Rose*?

   a) Milton Berle
   b) Howard Cosell
   c) Sammy Davis, Jr.
   d) Tony Roberts

7. Who is Lou Canova's wife?

   a) Maria
   b) Marlene
   c) Terry
   d) Herbert

8. Who is Tina's old boyfriend?

    a) Carmine Rispoli
    b) Johnny Rispoli
    c) Topo Gigio
    d) Frank Sinatra

9. True or false:

    a) Lou Canova got his big break at the
        Copacabana.
    b) Herb Reynolds played Barney Dunn.
    c) Guilt is important because it keeps you
        from doing terrible things.
    d) For an eight-dollar tip Danny could have
        slept with the waitress.
    e) Herbie Jayson was a balloon folder.

10. Lou Canova did a guest appearance on which
    show?

    a) "Johnny Carson Show"
    b) "Joe Franklin Show"
    c) "Family Feud"
    d) "Uncle Floyd Show"

11. The Danny Rose fomula for curing "drunken-
    ness" includes: two aspirin, tomato juice,
    worcestershire sauce, goat cheese and what?

    a) Chicken fat
    b) Egg yolks
    c) Muenster cheese
    d) Shrimp brine

12. Who was the world's worst ventriloquist?

    a) Eddie Clark
    b) Barney Dunn
    c) Herbie Jayson
    d) Shandar

13. Johnny Rispoli tried to kill himself by swallowing what?

    a) Barbiturates
    b) Codliver oil
    c) Hoboken tap water
    d) Iodine

14. Match the description with the appropriate relative:

    a) Famous diabetic from Brooklyn
    b) Looked like something you'd buy in a live bait store
    c) Looked like something in a reptile house at the zoo
    d) Lovely uncle, dead completely

    Aunt Rose   Uncle Morris
    Cousin Ceil   Uncle Sidney

15. What place gives Tina "the creeps"?

    a) Atlantic City
    b) Beverly Hills
    c) California
    d) Las Vegas

16. Who said "I never forget my friends"?

    a) Lou Canova
    b) Barney Dunn
    c) Danny Rose
    d) Tina Vitale

17. Which of the following acts doesn't Danny manage?

    a) Balloon folders
    b) Barney Dunn
    c) One-armed juggler
    d) One-legged tap dancer

18. What was Lou's wife?

    a) Cocktail waitress
    b) Department store clerk
    c) Exotic dancer
    d) Racetrack cashier

19. How long did Lou Canova have a "hit" on the charts?

    a) A day and a half
    b) Fifteen minutes
    c) Three weeks
    d) Never had a hit

20. Pee Wee pecked out what song?

    a) "Agita"
    b) "My Funny Valentine"
    c) "September Song"
    d) "You're Nobody Till Somebody Loves You"

21. "You little cheese-eater" can be considered a homage to what movie gangster?

   a) Humphrey Bogart
   b) James Cagney
   c) George Raft
   d) Edward G. Robinson

22. Danny told Tina that he's never going to be:

   a) Gary Cooper
   b) Cary Grant
   c) Rock Hudson
   d) Jimmy Stewart

23. Who raised hamsters?

   a) Phil Chomsky
   b) Danny's father
   c) Uncle Menaghem
   d) Uncle Sidney

24. Danny represents a parrot that sings what song?

   a) "As Time Goes By"
   b) "I've Got to Be Me"
   c) "Moon River"
   d) "Stardust"

25. Danny tells Lou to sing "My Funny Valentine" with special lyrics about the:

   a) Jonestown Massacre
   b) Moon Landing
   c) Nuremberg Trial
   d) Watergate Investigation

26. Who isn't in the Thanksgiving Day Parade?

    a) Milton Berle
    b) Howard Cosell
    c) Sammy Davis, Jr.
    d) Ricky Schroeder

27. Eddie Clark's penguin skated on stage:

    a) And sang "Winchester Cathedral"
    b) Dressed like a rabbi
    c) Wearing a surgical mask
    d) With the Ice Capades

28. Who owned a fleet of cement trucks?

    a) Uncle Benny
    b) Uncle Johnny
    c) Uncle Rocco
    d) Uncle Vinny

29. What's the fortune teller's name?

    a) Angelina
    b) Danielle
    c) Sister Rose
    d) Zelda

30. How old is Johnny?

    a) 30
    b) 35
    c) 40
    d) 50

31.   At the Carnegie Deli, the sandwich that made Danny Rose famous consists of what ingredients?

a) Cream cheese on a bagel with marinara
b) Lotsa corned beef and lotsa pastrami
c) Chopped liver, hard boiled egg and onion
d) Hot Virginia ham and candied sweets

32.   Tina Vitale and Ray Webb went to what restaurant on their first date?

a) Clarke's on Third Avenue
b) Elaine's on Second Avenue
c) The Russian Tea Room on 57th Street
d) The Saloon on Broadway

33.   Barney Dunn was taken to what hospital?

a) Bellevue
b) Metropolitan
c) Roosevelt
d) Sloane

34.   At what diner did Danny's car get demolished?

35.   What is the name of the boat that Danny and Tina take across the Hudson?

Broadway Danny Rose
Answers

1.   b)   Jack Rollins, Jackie Gayle and Corbett Monica

2.   d)   Have to sell storm windows

3.   a)   Uncle Sidney   c)   Uncle Morris
         b)   Aunt Rose   d)   Danny's father

4.   b)   Being shot in the back

5.   a)   Carnegie Deli

6.   d)   Tony Roberts

7.   c)   Terry

8.   b)   Johnny Rispoli

9. a) False   d) True
    b) True   e) False
    c) True

10. b) "Joe Franklin Show"

11. a) Chicken fat

12. b) Barney Dunn

13. d) Iodine

14. a) Uncle Morris   c) Cousin Ceil
     b) Aunt Rose   d) Uncle Sidney

15. c) California

16. a) Lou Canova

17. b) Barney Dunn

18. a) Cocktail waitress

19. b) Fifteen minutes

20. c) "September Song"

21. b) James Cagney

22. b) Cary Grant

23. c) Uncle Menaghem

24. b) "I've Got to Be Me"

25.   b) Moon Landing

26.   b) Howard Cosell

27.   b) Dressed like a rabbi

28.   c) Uncle Rocco

29.   a) Angelina

30.   c) 40

31.   b) Lotsa corned beef and lotsa pastrami

32.   a) Clarke's on Third Avenue

33.   c) Roosevelt

34.   The Liberty View Diner

35.   Freddy K.

Zelig
Questions

1. True or false:

    a) Santo Loquasto was nominated for an Oscar for Costume Design.
    b) Eudora Fletcher has a sister Merl.
    c) The KKK considered Zelig a double threat.
    d) Gordon Willis won an Academy Award for Cinematography.
    e) Zelig delivered a baby with ice tongs.

2. On his death bed, Morris Zelig's only advice to his son was to what?

    a) Fondle his nurse
    b) Marry a horse
    c) Read *Moby Dick*
    d) Save string

3.   Zelig posed as which of the following?

a) A fur trapper
b) An actor
c) The brother of Duke Ellington
d) All of the above

4.   What was the name of the hospital at which Zelig was a patient?

a) Beekman
b) Manhattan
c) Mount Sinai
d) Roosevelt

5.   Who was the strange visitor to the Yankee training camp?

a) Babe Zelig
b) Henry Zelig
c) Lou Zelig
d) Rocky Zelig

6.   The narrator in *Zelig* was:

a) Jackson Beck
b) Patrick Horgan
c) Don Pardo
d) Mario Cuomo

7.   Who gave Zelig the New York City Medal of Valor?

a) Carter Dean
b) Ed Koch
c) Jimmy Walker
d) Vito Corleone

8.   Which of the following songs were in *Zelig*?

     a)   "Leonard the Lizard"
     b)   "Reptile Eyes"
     c)   "You're Six People, But I Love You"
     d)   All of the above

9.   Zelig was sued for bigamy, adultery, automobile accidents, plagiarism, household damages, negligence, property damage and what else?

     a)   Collaborating with an owl
     b)   Fraud
     c)   Performing unnecessary dental extractions
     d)   Shaving gerbils

10. Zelig's illness was diagnosed as what?

     a)   A brain tumor
     b)   A result of eating Mexican food
     c)   Mental in origin
     d)   a and b
     e)   All of the above

11. A billboard shows Zelig saying what?

     a)   Do the Chameleon
     b)   We Smoke Camels
     c)   I'm Capable of Infinite Orgasms
     d)   I Can Go Out with You Alone, but You Can Come with Any of Me

12. Those interviewed in *Zelig* include:

    a) Susan Sontag and Saul Bellow
    b) Zelda and Scott Fitzgerald
    c) Clara Bow and the entire Southern Cal football team
    d) Jack Benny and Rochester

13. Who wrote the lyrics for "Leonard the Lizard"?

    a) Woody Allen
    b) Burt Bacharach
    c) Marvin Hamlisch
    d) Dick Hyman

14. Zelig was photographed with what President?

    a) Calvin Coolidge
    b) Franklin Roosevelt
    c) Teddy Roosevelt
    d) Woodrow Wilson

15. What is the title of the Warner Bros. version of Zelig's life?

    a) *Lynch the Little Heeb*
    b) *The Changing Man*
    c) *The Innocent Man*
    d) *The Ultimate Conformist*

16. Leonard has to get back to town because he teaches a class. Where?

    a) Brandeis
    b) Masters and Johnson
    c) The Psychiatric Institute
    d) None of the above

17. What course does he claim to teach?

   a) Advanced masturbation
   b) Group masturbation
   c) Guilt-ridden masturbation
   d) Oral calligraphy

18. He's concerned that if he doesn't get back to town soon:

   a) All the good seats will be taken
   b) Class will start without him
   c) He would have to begin alone
   d) He wouldn't be able to get a grip on himself.

19. With whom does Zelig hobnob at San Simeon?

   a) Marion Davies
   b) Tom Mix
   c) Jimmy Walker
   d) All of the above

20. The atrocities that Zelig performed under a different personality included what?

   a) Defrauding National Life Insurance Co.
   b) Painting someone's house a disgusting color
   c) To perform unnecessary liver surgery
   d) All of the above

Zelig
Answers

1. a) True   d) False
    b) True   e) True
    c) False

2. d) Save string

3. d) All of the above

4. b) *Manhattan*

5. c) Lou Zelig

6. b) Patrick Horgan

7. a) Carter Dean

8. d) All of the above

9. c) Performing unnecessary dental extractions

10. e) All of the above

11. b) We smoke Camels

12. a) Susan Sontag and Saul Bellow

13. d) Dick Hyman

14. a) Calvin Coolidge

15. b) *The Changing Man*

16. c) The Psychiatric Institute

17. a) Advanced masturbation

18. b) Class will start without him

19. d) All of the above

20. b) Painting someone's house a disgusting color

Purple Rose of Cairo
Questions

1. What was the name of the theatre that was showing *The Purple Rose of Cairo*?

    a) Beekman
    b) Belmont
    c) Jewel
    d) West Bank

2. When does *The Purple Rose of Cairo* take place?

    a) 1920's   c) 1940's
    b) 1930's   d) 1950's

3. What was the name of Danny Aiello's character?

    a) Gil   c) Monk
    b) Larry   d) Zoe

4. Where does *The Purple Rose of Cairo* take place?

   a) Connecticut   c) New York
   b) New Jersey   d) Rhode Island

5. For what categories did *The Purple Rose of Cairo* receive Academy Award nominations?

   a) Best Director   d) a and b
   b) Best Picture   e) Received no
   c) Best Screenplay   nominations

6. What explanation does a character in the audience give for the miracle of Tom Baxter scampering off the screen?

   a) "In Jersey, anything can happen."
   b) "It's a figment of your imagination."
   c) "It's that new-fangled 3-D."
   d) "Trick photography."

7. What Woody Allen short-story does *The Purple Rose of Cairo* call to mind?

   a) "By Destiny Denied"
   b) "Examining Psychic Phenomena"
   c) "Mr. Big"
   d) "The Kugelmass Episode"

8. To what club are the characters going while in New York?

   a) Copacabana   c) Nell's
   b) El Morroco   d) Palladium

9. Who portrayed the Tom Baxter character during the initial filming?

   a) Dan Ackroyd   c) Michael Keaton
   b) Chevy Chase   d) Steve Martin

10. Match the actor with his or her character:

   a) Stephanie Farrow
   b) Edward Hermann
   c) Van Johnson
   d) Deborah Rush
   e) Diane Wiest
   f) John Wood

   Cecilia's sister   Jason
   Emma   Larry
   Henry   Rita

Purple Rose of Cairo
Answers

1.   c) Jewel

2.   b) 1930's

3.   c) Larry

4.   b) New Jersey

5.   c) Best Screenplay

6.   a) "In New Jersey, anything can happen."

7.   d) "The Kugelmass Episode"

8.   a) Copacabana

9.   c) Michael Keaton

10. a) Cecilia's sister   d) Rita
     b) Henry   e) Emma
     c) Larry   f) Jason

Hannah and Her Sisters
Questions

1. Mickey was "lucky to run into Holly" at which record store?

   a) Colony   c) Sam Goody
   b) King Karol   d) Tower Records

2. What is the opening song in *Hannah and Her Sisters*?

   a) "Bewitched"
   b) "I'm in Love Again"
   c) "The Way You Look Tonight"
   d) "You Made Me Love You"

3. What does Hannah think is the cause of Mickey's infertility?

   a) Excessive masturbation
   b) Too few push-ups
   c) Lack of vitamins
   d) Bad hormones

153

4. Sam Waterson, who plays David, also appears in what other Allen film?

   a) *Bananas*
   b) *Interiors*
   c) *The Purple Rose of Cairo*
   d) *Zelig*

5. What is David's profession?

   a) Architect
   b) Dentist
   c) Engineer
   d) Lawyer

6. In which of Woody's other films did Daniel Stern (Dusty) also appear?

   a) *Annie Hall*
   b) *Manhattan*
   c) *Radio Days*
   d) *Stardust Memories*

7. Where did Lee take classes?

   a) Brooklyn College
   b) City College
   c) Columbia University
   d) NYU

8. What's the name of the priest who introduces Catholicism?

   a) Cardinal O'Connor
   b) Father Flynn
   c) Father O'Malley
   d) Father Mulcahy

9. Mickey has been doing all of his own reading since when?

   a) He joined the Catholic faith
   b) He quit television
   c) Since he was thirty
   d) Since he was forty

10. What theater did Mickey walk into when he was trying to get his thoughts into rational perspective?

    a) Cinema Studio   c) Olympia
    b) Metro   d) Thalia

11. What Marx Brothers movie was playing?

    a) *A Night at the Opera*
    b) *Coconuts*
    c) *Duck Soup*
    d) *Horsefeathers*

12. Who used to "knock off" little Greek boys?

    a) Aristotle   c) Plato
    b) Nietzsche   d) Socrates

13. To what bookstore does Holly take Elliot?

    a) Applause   c) Pageant
    b) Gotham   d) Gryphon

14. Match the scene with the song:

    a) Mickey and Holly strolling through Central Park
    b) Elliot and Lee at the bookstore

c) Hannah's apartment Thanksgiving night
d) Holly and Mickey at the Carlyle
e) Evan and Norma's apartment
f) Mickey leaving the doctor's office
g) The waterfront at dusk

"Back to the Apple"
"Bewitched"
"Concerto in F Minor"
"I'm in Love Again"
"It Could Happen to You"
"You are Too Beautiful"
"You Made Me Love You"

15. What sketch does Standards and Practice not allow to air?

a) Cardinal Spellman—Ronald Reagan Homosexual Dance Number
b) Child Molestation with the Pope
c) PLO
d) None of the above

16. Match the saying with the character:

a) "Of course there's a God, you idiot!"
b) "It's probably my fault. I've been a little depressed lately."
c) "The point is—we need some sperm."
d) "Can you imagine the level of the mind that watches wrestling?"

Frederick   Holly   Mickey   Mother

17. David shows Holly & April the following landmark building:

    a) Avon Building
    b) Citicorp Center
    c) Dakota
    d) Empire State Building

18. At the conclusion of *Hannah and Her Sisters,* Evan plays what song on the piano?

    a) I'm in Love Again
    b) Isn't It Romantic
    c) The Way You Look Tonight
    d) You Made Me Love You

19. What was the name of the bank at Downtown Beirut?

    a) Fine Young Cannibals
    b) Midnight Oil
    c) Ninety-Nine Steps
    d) The Cure

20. Who was the performer at the Carlyle?

    a) Michael Feinstein
    b) Johnny Mathis
    c) Brian Rago
    d) Bobby Short

Hannah and Her Sisters
Answers

1.   d)   Tower Records

2.   d)   "You Made Me Love You"

3.   a)   Excessive masturbation

4.   b)   *Bananas*

5.   a)   Architect

6.   d)   *Stardust Memories*

7.   c)   Columbia University

8.   b)   Father Flynn

9.   d)   Since he was forty

10. c) Olympia

11. c) *Duck Soup*

12. d) Socrates

13. c) Pageant

14. a) "You Made Me Love You"
     b) "Bewitched"
     c) "It Could Happen to You"
     d) "I'm in Love Again"
     e) "You Are Too Beautiful"
     f) "Back to the Apple"
     g) "Concerto in F Minor"

15. b) Child molestation with the Pope

16. a) Mother   c) Mickey
     b) Holly   d) Frederick

17. c) the Dakota

18. b) Isn't It Romantic

19. c) Ninety-Nine Steps

20. d) Bobby Short

Radio Days
Questions

1. In *Radio Days'* opening scene, whose house gets robbed?

   a) The Berkowitz'
   b) The Neddlebaums'
   c) The Rothmans'
   d) The Waldbaums'

2. Match the family members with their favorite radio show:

   a) "Bill Kern's Favorite Sports Legends"
   b) "Breakfast with Irene and Roger"
   c) "The Famous Ventriloquist"

   Abe   Ceil   Mom

3. To what song do Ruthie and the girls "swoon"?

   a) "All or Nothing at all"
   b) "I Don't Want to Walk without You"
   c) "I'll Be Seeing You"
   d) "Paper Doll"

4.   Who hosts "The Court of Human Emotions"?

a)   Thomas Abercrombie
b)   Herbie Hanson
c)   Kyle Kirby
d)   Sidney Manulis

5.   Wallace Shawn, who portrays the Masked Avenger, appears in what other Woody Allen film?

a)   *Annie Hall*
b)   *Manhattan*
c)   *Take the Money and Run*
d)   *Zelig*

6.   Who is the Danny Aiello character that bumps off Mr. Davis?

a)   Antonio   c)   Rocco
b)   Guido   d)   Tony

7.   Who ran into the street wielding a meat cleaver?

a)   Mr. Phelps   c)   Mr. Waldbaum
b)   Mr. Silverman   d)   Mr. Zipsky

8.   Hy Ansell (Mr. Waldbaum) appears in what other Woody Allen film?

a)   *Annie Hall*   c)   *The Front*
b)   *Interiors*   d)   *September*

9.   Who was Bea's "effeminate" date?

a)   Brian   c)   Fred
b)   Bruce   d)   Wally

10. What is Ruthie to Little Joe?

    a) Brother   c) Sister
    b) Cousin   d) No relation

11. Who played the bandleader in the King Cole's Room?

    a) Xavier Cugat   c) Ricky Riccardo
    b) Tito Puente   d) Carlos Sanchez

12. Who was Bea's date when she won the Silver Dollar Jackpot?

    a) Chester   c) Mr. Manilus
    b) Fred   d) Sy

13. Gian DeAngelis (Mama) appeared in what other Woody Allen film?

    a) *A Midsummer's Night Sex Comedy*
    b) *Broadway Danny Rose*
    c) *The Front*
    d) *Zelig*

14. Which nightclub did Mr. Davis own?

    a) Copacabana   c) King Cole Room
    b) El Morocco   d) Palladium

15. What was the name of the musical game show?

    a) "Guess That Tune"
    b) "Name That Song"
    c) "What's That Tune"
    d) "Who Sings That"

16. Michael Tucker (Pop) appears in what other Allen movie?

    a) *A Midsummer's Night Sex Comedy*
    b) *Broadway Danny Rose*
    c) *Stardust Memories*
    d) *The Purple Rose of Cairo*

17. According to Abe, who goes out on New Year's Eve?

    a) Everyone
    b) Just morons
    c) Only creeps and crazy people
    d) Starcrazed lunatics

18. Abe wants to celebrate New Year's with what type of fish?

    a) Catfish   c) Red snapper
    b) Fluke   d) Sea bass

19. How much did the Masked Avenger Secret Compartment ring cost?

    a) 10 cents   c) 25 cents
    b) 15 cents   d) $1.00

20. What exciting new actor played Kirby Kyle?

    a) Tom Cruise   c) Brian Mannain
    b) Brian Hamill   d) Brian Rago

21. What did "Pop" do for a living?

    a) Drove a cab
    b) Manufactured greeting cards
    c) Sold mail order jewelry
    d) Wholesaled cultured pearls

22. Match the lines with their characters:

    a) "Beware evildoers, wherever you are."
    b) "If you don't like it, take the gas pipe."
    c) "One American with courage is worth twenty of you."
    d) "That's too good for him, he deserves an enema."
    e) "It's different, our lives are ruined already."
    f) "You speak the truth my faithful Indian companion."
    g) "Who is Pearl Harbor?"

    Abe   Mom
    Biff Baxter   Sally
    Ceil   The Masked Avenger
    Little Joe

23. What is the name of Diane Keaton's character?

24. What's the name of his character in that film?

25. Which student displayed his "Masked Avenger" ring during "Show and Tell"?

    a) Andrew   c) Little Arnold
    b) Burt   d) Little Ross

Radio Days
Answers

1.   b) The Needlebaums'

2.   a) Abe
       b) Mom
       c) Ceil

3.   a) "All or Nothing at All"

4.   a) Thomas Abercrombie

5.   b) *Manhattan*

6.   c) Rocco

7.   d) Mr. Zipsky

8.   a) *Annie Hall*

9.   c) Fred

10.   b) Cousin

11.   b) Tito Puente

12.   d) Sy

13.   b) *Broadway Danny Rose*

14.   b) El Morocco

15.   a) "Guess That Tune"

16.   d) *The Purple Rose of Cairo*

17.   c) Only creeps and crazy people

18.   c) Red snapper

19.   b) 15 cents

20.   c) Brian Mannain

21.   a) Drove a cab

22.   a) The Masked Avenger
      b) Abe
      c) Biff Baxter
      d) Ceil
      e) Mom
      f) Little Joe
      g) Sally

23.   Monica Charles

24.   Joey Nichols

25.   d) Little Ross

September Questions

1. Match the actors with their characters:

    a) Denholm Elliott   Diane
    b) Mia Farrow   Howard
    c) Elaine Stritch   Lane
    d) Jack Warden   Lloyd
    e) Sam Waterston   Peter
    f) Diane Wiest   Stephanie

2. Who was originally cast as Lloyd?

    a) Charles Durning
    b) Denholm Elliott
    c) Sam Shepard
    d) Christopher Walken

3. In the initial filming, who was the "aspiring" writer?

    a) Robert DeNiro
    b) Sean Penn
    c) Sam Shepard
    d) Christopher Walken

4. Who was originally cast as "the neighbor"?

    a) Charles Durning
    b) Denholm Elliott
    c) Jack Nicholson
    d) Jack Warden

5. Who played "mother" the first time around?

    a) Bea Arthur
    b) Maureen O'Hara
    c) Maureen O'Sullivan
    d) Elaine Stritch

6. Where was *September* filmed?

    a) Kaufman Studio
    b) Mia's country home
    c) Mia's New York apartment
    d) Vermont

7. Who was unable to participate in the second filming of *September* due to previous commitments?

    a) Charles Durning
    b) Robert Duvall
    c) Gene Hackman
    d) Jack Warden

8.   *September* came in:

   a)   at budget
   b)   below budget
   c)   10% above budget
   d)   20% above budget

9.   These two songs can be heard on
   the *September* soundtrack:

   a)   Body & Soul/Goodbye (Benny Goodman)
   b)   Night & Day/What'll I Do
        (Irving Berlin)
   c)   September Song/I've Heard That Song
        Before (Harry James)
   d)   You Took Advantage of Me/Little
        Girl Blue (L. Hart-R. Rodgers)

10.   Stephanie's husband lives in what city?

   a)   Atlanta
   b)   Chicago
   c)   New York
   d)   Philadelphia

September
Answers

1. a) Howard   d) Lloyd
    b) Lane   e) Peter
    c) Diane   f) Stephanie

2. b) Denholm Elliot

3. c) Sam Shepard

4. a) Charles Durning

5. c) Maureen O'Sullivan

6. a) Kaufman Studio

7. a) Charles Durning

8. d) 20 percent above budget

9. d) Philadelphia

10. b) Night and day/What'll I Do

Another Woman/Oedipus Wrecks
Crimes and Misdemeanors

Match the stars with their characters

1.	Sandy Dennis	a)	Claire
2.	Mia Farrow	b)	Hope
3.	Gene Hackman	c)	Ken
4.	Ian Holm	d)	Laura
5.	John Houseman	e)	Larry
6.	Martha Plimpton	f)	Marion
7.	Gena Rowlands	g)	Marion's father

8. The soundtrack includes a song that is also heard in what other film?

   a) As Time Goes By *(Play It Again, Sam)*
   b) He Loves And She Loves *(Manhattan)*
   c) Seems Like Old Times *(Annie Hall)*
   d) You'd Be So Nice To Come Home To *(Radio Days)*

9.   Who makes the statement "There are times when even a historian shouldn't look at the past?"

    a) Ken
    b) Larry
    c) Marion
    d) Marion's father

10.   What actress played the ex-wife of Ken?

    a) Betty Buckley   c) Blythe Danner
    b) Frances Conroy d) Mia Farrow

11.   What was the "theme" song from *Oepidus Wrecks?*

    a) A Fine Romance
    b) All the Things You Are
    c) I Want a Girl Just Like the Girl That Married Dear Old Dad
    d) You Made Me Love You

12.   What is Sheldon's profession?

    a) Accountant   c) Corporate Lawyer
    b) Banker   d) Stock Broker

Match the actor with their character:

13.   Lisa   a) Woody Allen
14.   Mother b) Mia Farrow
15.   Sheldon c) Julie Kavner
16.   Treva   d) Mae Questel

17. What character says "it's funny, you wake
    up one day and your're not in love anymore."

    a) Lisa
    b) Mother
    c) Sheldon
    d) Treva

18. How did mother describe Sheldon's boss?

    a) He's likes to break wind.
    b) He's the cheapskate.
    c) He's the one with a mistress.
    d) He's the one with bad breath.

19. What play did mother see prior to
    visiting Sheldon?

    a) *Cats*
    b) *Legs Diamond*
    c) *Oh Calcutta!*
    d) *Phantom of the Opera*

20. What is Sheldon's real last name?

    a) Johnson
    b) Millstein
    c) Rabbi Harry Sharpstein
    d) Weinstein

Another Woman/Oedipus Wrecks
Crimes and Misdemeanors

Match the character with the phrase

21. If it bends its funny, if it breaks – it's not funny.

22. The last time I was inside a woman is when I visited the Statue of Liberty.

23. I went out the window.

24. What would I do with a hand full of putty?

   a) Cliff
   b) Halley
   c) Lester
   d) Professor Levy

25. Match the actor with his character

   Alan Alda   Martin Landau
   Woody Allen   Jerry Orbach

   a) Cliff
   b) Jack
   c) Judah
   d) Lester

26.   What was Cliff's worst nightmare realized?

   a)   Halley falling in love with Lester.
   b)   His sister responding to the personal ads.
   c)   Professor Levy committing suicide.
   d)   Spending an evening with an
        insurance salesman.

27.   Which one of the following films did
        Cliff see?

   a)   Angels with Dirty Faces
   b)   The Enforcer
   c)   The Roaring Twenties
   d)   This Gun For Hire

28.   Cliff remembers the date he last had
        sex because:

   a)   He just turned 40.
   b)   It was Hitler's birthday.
   c)   Lester had offered him a job.
   d)   That was when he won honorable
        mention for his documentary.

29.   Lester says that comedy is:

   a)   dog-eat-dog
   b)   dog-doesn't-return-other-dog's-
        phone-calls
   c)   tragedy plus time
   d)   all of the above

30.   Judah's profession:

a)   analologist
b)   ophtalmologist
c)   psychologist-gynecologist
d)   rabbi

Another Woman/Oedipus Wrecks
Crimes and Misdemeanors

1.   a)   Claire

2.   b)   Hope

3.   e)   Larry

4.   c)   Ken

5.   g)   Marion's father

6.   d)   Laura

7.   f)   Marion

8.   d)   You'd Be So Nice to Come Home To

9.   d)   Marion's Father

10.   a)   Betty Buckley

11.   c)   I Want A Girl

12.   c)   Corporate Lawyer

13.   b)   Mia Farrow

14.   d)   Mae Questel

15.   a)   Woody Allen

16.   c)   Julie Kavner

17.   a)   All the Things You Are

18.   c)   He's the one having an affair

19.   a)   Cats

20.   b)   Millstein

21.   c)   Lester

22.   a)   Cliff

23.   d)   Professor Levy

24.   b)   Halley

25.
Alan Alda   d)   Lester
Woody Allen   a)   Cliff
Martin Landau   c)   Judah
Jerry Orbach   b)   Jack

26.   a)   Halley falling in love with Lester

27.   d)   This Gun For Hire

28.   b)   it was Hitler's birthday

29.   c)   tragedy plus time

30.   b)   ophtalmologist

184

Personal Information Questions

1. Woody's CBS TV special featured:

    a) Candice Bergen, Billy Graham and the Fifth Dimension
    b) Louis Lasser, Billy Graham and Dionne Warwick
    c) Barbara Feldon, Jerry Falwell and The Dave Clark Five
    d) Eva Braun, Rev. Moon and The Chicago Seven

2. "The Humor and Politics of Woody Allen" was withdrawn from Public T.V.:

    a) April 8, 1970
    b) April 3, 1971
    c) February 11, 1972
    d) February 23, 1981

3. Who provides his cousin's orgasmic insurance?

   a) Mutual of NY
   b) Mutual of Omaha
   c) Kennel Club of America
   d) Cadillac Dog Food Corporation

4. Woody drove the Moose down which roadway?

   a) Madison Avenue
   b) Long Island Expressway
   c) West Side Highway
   d) NJ Turnpike

5. Where was Woody's first nightclub appearance?

   a) Bon Soir   c) Duplex
   b) Bottom Line   d) Ramrod

6. What did Woody tell Billy Graham his greatest sin was?

   a) Getting married
   b) Getting divorced
   c) Having impure thoughts about Art Linkletter
   d) Voting for Richard Nixon

7. True or false—Woody:

   a) Performed at the Red Angel Lounge
   b) Once had his shoes shined against his will
   c) Was breastfed through falsies
   d) Appeared at Caesar's Palace in Las Vegas in 1966
   e) Placed his first wife under a pedestal
   f) The Ox Bow Incident refers to Woody's second marriage.

186

8.   When Woody was in the army, his leader was:

a) A Mexican hairless
b) An idiot
c) Gomer Pyle
d) Sergeant O'Rourke

9.   On which of the following shows was Woody
once a guest?

a) "Bob Hope Special"
b) "Gene Kelly Special"
c) "Mr. Ed"
d) "Smothers Brothers Show"

10.   Which cartoonist did the *Inside Woody Allen*
comic strip?

a) Stuart Hemple   c) Charles Schultz
b) Gary Larsen   d) Gary Trudeau

11.   With whom did Woody once do a vodka
advertisement?

a) Diane Keaton
b) Marilyn Monroe
c) Mamie Van Dooren
d) Monique Van Vooren

12.   When his rabbi tried to break into show
business by being on a late night prayer show,
he panicked when asked to name the Ten Com-
mandments and was only able to name:

a) The Beatles
b) Members of the Third Reich
c) The starting lineup of the NY Knicks
d) The Seven Dwarfs

13. Who was the special guest on Woody's 1970 TV special?

    a) Charles K. Feldman
    b) Boris Karloff
    c) Liza Minelli
    d) Leon Tolstoy

14. Who stepped on Woody's dog "Spot"?

    a) Brutus
    b) Sheldon Finkelstein
    c) Uri Geller
    d) Rabbi Rosenblum

15. What was "His Own Boswell"?

    a) A story in *Getting Even*
    b) A 1963 story about Woody Allen
    c) An Ingmar Bergman documentary
    d) A cartoon character drawn by Woody as a youth

16. What is Woody's Jazz Band called?

    a) The New Orleans Funeral and Ragtime Orchestra
    b) The New Orleans Ragtime Band
    c) The Original New York Ragtime Band
    d) The New Orleans Ragtime Rascals

17. Woody once compared Mort Sahl comedy to:

    a) Willie Mays in baseball
    b) Charlie Parker in jazz
    c) Walt Frazier in basketball
    d) Ingmar Bergman in film

18. As a youth, where did Woody live?

a) 262 Central Park West
b) Coney Island Blvd., Brooklyn
c) Avenue K and 15th St., Brooklyn
d) Babylon, Long Island

19. True or false:

a) Woody's first public clarinet performance in NYC was at Barney Googles on 86th Street.
b) "How Humphrey Bogart Made Me the Superb Lover I am Today" was the working title of *Play It Again, Sam.*
c) *"Please Pray for Woody Allen"* by H.M. Conn was written for the Christian Science Monitor.

20) When was Woody born?

a) January 25, 1954
b) March 9, 1939
c) December 1, 1935
d) All of the above

21. According to "legend" what is his real name?

a) Heywood Allen III
b) Woodrow Wilson Allen
c) Allen Stewart Konigsberg
d) Rabbi Henry Sharpstein

22. What do Woody's parents value?

a) Buying wholesale
b) God and carpeting
c) Guilt and loathing
d) Job security

23. What magazine voted Woody one of the ten sexiest men in America?

    a) *Christian Science Monitor*
    b) *Field and Stream*
    c) *Playgirl*
    d) *Popular Mechanics*

24. The first Woody Allen comedy album was released on:

    a) Capital—1963
    b) Colpix—1964
    c) Columbia—1964
    d) Polygram—1962

25. "A Loser on Top" appeared November 22, 1963, in what magazine?

    a) *Esquire*
    b) *Newsweek*
    c) *Senior Scholastic*
    d) *Orgasm*

26. Which of the following singers was once Woody's opening act?

    a) Jim Croce   c) Bobby Short
    b) John Denver   d) Mel Torme

27. At seventeen, Woody was writing jokes for which comedian?

    a) Mel Brooks   c) Buster Keaton
    b) Sid Caesar   d) Herb Shriner

28.   As a teenager, Woody wrote approximately how many jokes in two years?

a) 500   c) 10,000
b) 1,000   d) 25,000

29.   Woody and Mia recently had:

a) A boy   c) One of each
b) A girl   d) All of the above

30.   What is the child's name?

a) Alison
b) Satchel
c) Satchmo
d) Rabbi Henry Sharpstein

Personal Information
Answers

1. a) Candice Bergen, Billy Graham and the Fifth Dimension

2. c) February 11, 1972

3. b) Mutual of Omaha

4. c) West Side Highway

5. c) Duplex

6. c) Having impure thoughts about Art Linkletter

7. a) False   d) True
    b) True   e) True
    c) True   f) False

8.   a) A Mexican hairless

9.   b) "Gene Kelly Special"

10. a) Stuart Hemple

11. d) Monique Van Vooren

12. d) The Seven Dwarves

13. c) Liza Minelli

14. b) Sheldon Finkelstein

15. b) A 1963 story about Woody Allen

16. a) The New Orleans Funeral and Ragtime
         Orchestra

17. b) Charlie Parker in jazz

18. c) Avenue K and 15th St., Brooklyn

19. a) True   b) False   c) True

20. c) December 1, 1935

21. c) Allen Stewart Konigsberg

22. b) God and carpeting

23. c) *Playgirl*

24.   b)   Colpix—1964

25.   c)   Senior Scholastic

26.   a)   Jim Croce

27.   d)   Herb Shriner

28.   d)   25,000

29.   a)   A boy

30.   b)   Satchel